Outsourcing IT

A Governance Guide

Outsourcing IT

A Governance Guide

RUPERT KENDRICK

IT Governance Publishing

Every possible effort has been made to ensure that the information contained in this book is accurate at the time of going to press, and the publishers and the author cannot accept responsibility for any errors or omissions, however caused. No responsibility for loss or damage occasioned to any person acting, or refraining from action, as a result of the material in this publication can be accepted by the publisher or the author.

The publisher and author have taken all reasonable care to ensure that all material in this book is original, is in the public domain, or is used with the permission of the original copyright owner. However, if any person believes that material for which they own the copyright has found its way into this book without permission, please contact the publisher who will investigate and remedy any inadvertent infringement.

Apart from any fair dealing for the purposes of research or private study, or criticism or review, as permitted under the Copyright, Designs and Patents Act 1988, this publication may only be reproduced, stored or transmitted, in any form, or by any means, with the prior permission in writing of the publisher or, in the case of reprographic reproduction, in accordance with the terms of licences issued by the Copyright Licensing Agency. Enquiries concerning reproduction outside those terms should be sent to the publishers at the following address:

IT Governance Publishing
IT Governance Limited
Unit 3, Clive Court
Bartholomew's Walk
Cambridgeshire Business Park
Ely
Cambridgeshire
CB7 4EH
United Kingdom

www.itgovernance.co.uk

© R. Kendrick 2009
The author has asserted the rights of the author under the Copyright, Designs and Patents Act, 1988, to be identified as the author of this work.

First published in the United Kingdom in 2009
by IT Governance Publishing.

ISBN 978-1-84928-025-9

FOREWORD

Writing this book has been, what I might term, a time-critical exercise. By this I mean that a constant challenge throughout has been the need to keep up to date with the many rapid changes that are emerging in IT outsourcing, particularly Cloud computing.

Subjects which I seemed to have covered were suddenly exposed to new ideas, thoughts and suggestions by leading commentators in the field. As one of my friends once put it, 'it's all changing so fast – faster than you can write it down!' I hope I have risen to the challenge adequately.

I must acknowledge the helpful guidance and contributions of others. In particular, my thanks go to: Tim Amatt, EquaTerra; Chris Cann, Martin Kaye & Co; Chris Cherrington, Capgemini; Alistair Maughan, Morrison & Foerster; Andy McCallum, SHL Group; Sean McDonough, ProActis; Chris Newton, Pemberton 4000; Andy Ross, SHL Group; Andrea Spiegelhoff, TPI; Dr Richard Sykes, independent strategic adviser and member of Intellect's main board; and Paul Vincent, Insight Sourcing Solutions, for helping me with interviews on specific issues, or with the provision of valuable background information.

I must also thank the publishers, IT Governance, for their patience and support, and all who have given permission for reproduction of their material.

Finally, thanks to my wife, Sonia, who has been very patient over the hours I have spent at my computer writing this book; and Hero, my Yorkshire Terrier, without whose help this book would have been finished very much sooner!

PREFACE

IT departments are under increasing pressure to meet the many, often conflicting, demands of boards of directors, shareholders, end-users and competitors to name but a few. The need to compete in a global market intensifies this pressure, bringing with it the need for: skilled personnel, regular upgrading or replacement of systems and networks, a proliferation of software licences, and even new premises – in other words, considerable cost.

In response to the need to identify specialist suppliers of IT services capable of responding with agility to fierce global competition with greater economy, many boards of directors have turned to outsourcing the IT function to specialist suppliers.

Statistics show that this trend is growing, but there is also a body of evidence to show that many IT outsourcing projects fail. The reasons are many and various, but almost all have their origins in inadequate adoption of governance processes and procedures.

The governance of any organisation is led by the board. The board sets the strategy. It embraces the principles of: transparent decision making; clear lines of responsibility and accountability; acknowledging shareholder and other stakeholder interests; risk management; and compliance, including information security. In the case of IT governance, there should be added – the need to ensure that IT projects remain aligned with the strategic objectives of the business.

Preface

IT governance principles are supported by various methodologies, most notably, PRINCE2®, and other tools, such as British, international and European standards, as well as various specialist trade and industry codes. Methodologies and tools are not in themselves governance. They simply support the application of governance principles.

This book addresses three components of the governance of IT outsourcing: the IT outsourcing process; the nature of governance and the use of methodologies and tools for the implementation of governance principles; and the management of risk within the IT outsourcing process.

Offshore IT outsourcing has been considered only briefly, with a short section on some key considerations as a subset to the overall subject of IT outsourcing. It is highly specialist and, in the context of governance, probably justifies research for another publication.

The research has also been confined to the private sector. Local and central government procurement is also highly specialist, with particularly complex EEC provisions governing procurement, and likewise is worthy of a separate publication.

The research is examined from the perspective of the organisation. Throughout the book, the party requiring outsourcing services is referred to as the organisation; and the provider of the service as the supplier. The objectives of the book are first, to provide boards of directors with clear criteria for the application of governance principles in an IT outsourcing environment; and, second, to provide guidance on useful strategies, processes and procedures for their implementation.

ABOUT THE AUTHOR

Rupert Kendrick is a non-practising solicitor and, for many years, was a partner in a medium-sized law firm.

For the past ten years, he has pursued a career in legal publishing, as an author, editor and columnist, also offering consultancy services, as director of a risk management consultancy, Web4Law Ltd, principally on IT issues.

He studied the implications of the Internet for law firm marketing strategies as part of a Masters programme in 1998 and his book *Managing Cyber-Risks*, which he is currently researching for a second edition, was published in 2002. He is a member of the Law Society's Technology and Legal Reference Group.

He has written, trained and consulted widely in the legal profession on legal and IT issues.

CONTENTS

Chapter 1: A governance overview 1
   Introduction 1
   Governance 4
   Risk 8
   Governance structures 10
   Managing the supplier relationship 14
   Cloud computing 16
   Governance structures 22
   Conclusion 25

Chapter 2: The in-house IT challenge 27
   The importance of IT 28
   IT functions 30
   Function analysis 30
   Performance challenges 32
   Conclusion 36

Chapter 3: Outsourcing considerations 37
   Definition 37
   Outsourcing trends 38
   General considerations 38
   IT considerations 41
   Objectives 48
   Stakeholders 50

Chapter 4: Reaching the decision 53
   Advantages 53
   Disadvantages 57
   Offshore outsourcing 62
   Conclusion 65

Chapter 5: Models of IT outsourcing 67
   IT outsourcing strategies 67
   Outsourcing models 68

Outsourced IT functions 78
Examples of outsourced IT functions 80
Conclusion 82
Chapter 6: Pre-contract procedures 85
Strategy objectives 86
Selection strategy 87
Due diligence 90
Tendering and negotiations 95
Chapter 7: The contract 101
Reasons for a contract 101
Contract construction 102
Multiple-outsourcing 108
Key success factors 111
Cloud computing contracts 113
Chapter 8: The service level agreement 119
Service levels 119
Scope 121
Pricing 122
SLA framework 122
Cloud computing SLAs 125
Chapter 9: Managing the contract, the SLA and the transition 127
Managing the contract 127
Managing the SLA 129
SLA relationships 135
Transition 143
Chapter 10: Contract change control 147
Reasons for change 147
Types of change 148
Considerations 149
Administration 149
Chapter 11: Contract exit 151
The contract term 151

Contents

Exit options 152
Managing the exit strategy 156
Disputes..157
Back-sourcing 163
Chapter 12: Corporate governance..............................169
Definition 171
Corporate governance frameworks 173
Chapter 13: IT governance 177
Definition 178
Criteria 178
Governance frameworks 181
Governance framework tools......................................187
IT governance and service management.....................199
Conclusion 202
Chapter 14: Project governance 205
Definition 205
Governance 207
Objectives 208
Project governance features 208
Project governance tools...210
Programme portfolio management 214
Project governance technology 218
Project management standards....................................219
Conclusion 220
Chapter 15: Risk assessment..223
Project failure..223
Risk assessment 226
The risk assessment...231
Chapter 16: Identifying the risks.................................235
Strategic and managerial risk......................................236
Technology risks...238
Compliance risks...239
Operational risks 240

Financial risks 242
  Cloud computing risks 244
  Conclusion 247
Chapter 17: Risk management structure 249
  Strategy principles 249
  Objectives and benefits 250
  Risk management framework 251
  The risk manager 252
  The risk management team 253
  Risk management standards 261
  Conclusion 264
Chapter 18: Risk management strategies 265
  Management of IT risks 265
  Management of legal and compliance risks 276
  Management of operational risks 289
  Management of financial risks 296
Chapter 19: Conclusion: the governance imperative . 307
  Conclusion 316
Bibliography 319
Further resources 320
ITG Resources 321

CHAPTER 1: A GOVERNANCE OVERVIEW

The drive towards outsourcing the IT function is a response to the emergence of a 'new' business environment. This new environment arises from the globalisation of world commerce and the consequent need for organisations not only to survive, but also to compete in a world-wide market.

Introduction

IT is a fundamental and essential tool for any organisation in meeting the demands of its customers in such a challenging marketplace. As important as understanding the importance of IT is the need to recognise how it should be acquired, deployed, managed and exploited for maximum business benefit and achievement of business objectives.

The traditional strategy has been to develop in-house IT facilities. However, many organisations have found this strategy to be resource-intensive, in terms of both finance and personnel, and often wanting in its ability to respond rapidly and flexibly to the needs of an ever-changing market – a market in which organisations have to meet highly demanding and specialist customer needs.

These drivers for more efficient and responsive IT are compounded by the current economic downturn which has thrown into focus the need to secure solutions that are not only efficient and responsive, but also allow a more effective and competitive use of resources.

1: A Governance Overview

Organisations are now more risk aware – and also risk averse. Many organisations have found an in-house IT function to be a management strategy too far. Legal and regulatory compliance issues are no longer national; they are global. Non-compliance in areas of information security and copyright infringement now have global consequences involving criminal and civil sanctions as well as the risk of damage to reputation in a global market. Additional demand for more resources to be allocated for managing the IT function comes at a time when the economic climate is already resulting in pressures on budgets.

These factors have led to the need for organisations to adopt a more rigorous approach to procurement of services, especially IT services, where effective performance is critical for survival. In the changing environment, the focus is now moving to outcomes. Complex supply chains are emerging in a market where a supplier can host services for an organisation, while, at the same time, outsourcing the hosting of those services to another hosting organisation.

Outsourcing the IT function in one form or another has been perceived as an effective strategy for achieving the business benefits that an in-house IT function should provide, but which, for whatever reason, it does not.

In some quarters, outsourcing the IT department has been seen as a panacea for organisations which find the challenge of managing an in-house function too daunting. This is especially the case in those organisations which do not embrace IT as a business tool, and where boards of directors have little appetite for addressing the need for an IT strategy and consequently offer no top-level commitment.

1: A Governance Overview

A decision to outsource the IT function goes to the heart of any organisation's business strategy. IT is an essential business tool for every organisation. Entrusting a business tool that is so critical to the survival and success of an organisation to a supplier about whom the organisation may know little or nothing carries significant risk. Many IT outsourcing projects benefit both organisation and supplier, but almost equally as many result in project failure. A principal reason for the high incidence of project failure is neglect by the organisation in addressing and managing adequately the process and risk that surround the project – in other words, neglecting to apply principles of governance.

The traditional IT outsourcing model involves a process of identifying how and why an outsourcing strategy should be adopted within the context of the organisation achieving its objectives and business goals. There follow processes of: supplier identification and selection; due diligence in tendering negotiation; contractual and service level agreement (SLA); transition, implementation and change control through contract management; and termination.

Each of these processes calls for systematic and focused strategic, managerial and operational skills to ensure that:

- the most suitable supplier is selected;
- the contract supports the organisation's business goals;
- the SLA provides levels of service that will satisfy the needs of the organisation's end-users; and that
- the project is implemented efficiently and effectively.

As outsourcing projects typically continue for several years and can involve many millions of pounds, the need for the organisation to ensure project success becomes critical.

1: A Governance Overview

Underpinning the actual mechanics of the transaction, several other issues arise:

- the project must have top-level support, or sponsorship;
- the interests of the stakeholders must be accommodated;
- the relationship with the supplier must be managed;
- strategic, IT, legal and compliance, operational and financial risks must be identified and managed.

IT outsourcing is a process of considerable complexity and significant risk which have the potential to destroy an organisation, either as a commercially viable entity, or simply in terms of its reputation. It requires principles of governance not only to be understood, but to be adopted, then rigorously applied.

Governance

In essence, governance is control and regulation implemented in such a way as to reflect good order. Three areas of governance need to be addressed in the context of an IT outsourcing contract: corporate governance, IT governance and project governance.

Corporate governance

Corporate governance is interpreted at board level as being conduct that includes: clearly defined responsibilities and line-management accountabilities; transparent decision making; taking account of the interests of shareholders and stakeholders; and addressing risk issues that include compliance and information security.

Outsourcing IT is a strategic decision for the organisation through which it aspires to improve its competitiveness and

1: A Governance Overview

its position in the marketplace. The initial decision to outsource must be made at board level because the strategy of any organisation is decided by the board.

Statutory and non-statutory frameworks prescribe the duties of directors in making strategic decisions, including, for instance, duties to: exercise reasonable care, due diligence and reasonable judgement; avoid conflict of interest; and declare interests.

The culture of corporate governance is set by the board and its principles should be promulgated to all levels of management.

IT governance

IT governance principles are a subset of corporate governance principles. They introduce a framework of leadership, structure, business processes, standards and compliance requirements designed to ensure that IT supports the achievement of the organisation's objectives.

Every organisation is different, but while the framework of leadership, organisational structures and business processes vary from organisation to organisation, the fundamental requirement that IT must support business objectives always remains.

Supporting this framework are various tools in the form of methodologies, standards and compliance legislation. It is often mistakenly believed that they are IT governance. They are not. They are tools by which IT governance is implemented.

This aspect of governance will be represented by the management infrastructure, including lines of responsibility, accountability and transparency, and decision-making processes at the various levels of the organisation; all of which will operate in the context of IT achieving business objectives.

Examples of the tools that may be used within the framework are: certification under relevant British, European or international standards addressing such issues as risk management, information security and data protection; or CobiT, which is an example of a methodology that is adopted within an IT governance framework.

One governance tool available to the board is ISO/IEC 38500:2008, a standard developed to provide directors and senior management of organisations with a set of key principles to be observed in achieving effective use of IT. It provides a clear and internationally recognisable model for the board's involvement in IT projects, of which outsourcing IT is a typical example. The standard addresses the interests of stakeholders, and provides guidance for directors in the evaluation of the corporate governance of IT. As well as the commercial benefits, it is also a valuable tool for risk management.

Project governance

Project governance is another subset of corporate governance. Here, governance principles address the development, implementation and conclusion of projects, of which outsourcing is a typical example.

The defining principles of project governance are: top-level leadership and oversight; a clear project plan with milestones; identification of resources; clear lines of responsibility, accountability reporting and communication; adoption of a recognised methodology for implementing the project; and a risk management strategy.

With such a variety of functions, this framework may involve several teams complementing the project team in fulfilling its responsibilities. For instance, in an outsourcing project, input may be necessary from teams concerned with transition, risk management, change control and management and a team to represent the retained IT function after completion of the project.

A framework of project governance may also be supported by various governance tools. Methodologies, such as PRINCE2® and tools, such as British, European or international standards are designed to assist in the management of projects within a governance framework.

Invariably, the IT department of an organisation will operate various different projects. This portfolio of projects also requires management within project governance principles. For example, an organisation may decide to outsource the provision of a small number of specialist IT applications, while leaving more general applications to be retained by the in-house IT department. This involves programme portfolio management (PPM). A clear risk of inadequately managed project portfolios is that the organisation's project strategy becomes aimless and confused, ultimately leading to project failure.

PPM is a process by which organisations prioritise, resource and implement a range of projects against governance principles and criteria, including: risk, business benefit, resources, and stakeholder interest. PPM is an essential governance feature of any project governance framework involving a range of IT projects.

1: A Governance Overview

Risk

These observations suggest a concept of governance that is akin to an ethos – a set of principles that represent good practice and business ethics to be applied right across the different functions of the management and administration of an organisation.

Properly applied, these principles are designed to ensure that the functions of an organisation are performed so as to achieve their business objectives, provide a return on investment and protect the interests of stakeholders.

Most crucially, the principles of governance also represent a comprehensive risk management tool that can be applied organisation-wide to every function. Governance provides a structured framework to an infrastructure that enhances the quality and transparency of decision making, through lines of responsibility from the board downwards, and lines of accountability from junior executives upwards; and so ensures that the results of decisions are monitored, audited and reviewed.

Risks abound in every IT outsourcing project. They range across strategy, IT, legal and regulatory compliance, operational functions and financial issues.

Effective corporate, IT and project governance structures, supported by methodologies and standards for their implementation, enable these risks to be assessed and managed systematically.

For instance, strategic concerns over a supplier's ability to provide adequate business continuity and disaster recovery services can be met by a requirement by the organisation at tendering stage that prospective suppliers should

1: A Governance Overview

demonstrate certification under relevant British, European or international standards.

Compliance concerns can be audited against relevant legal and regulatory provisions, such as the Data Protection Act 1998 (DPA) and Transfer of Undertaking and Protection of Employment Regulations 2006 (TUPE 2006) as well as industry specific codes of practice promulgated by, for instance, the Financial Services Authority (FSA).

Operational concerns, where a transfer of personnel is involved, can be checked against TUPE 2006 and, perhaps, any certification under the Investors in People standard.

Financial concerns can be audited against the audit requirements of audit standard SAS 70 published by the American Institute of Certified Public Accountants.

On their own, standards are evidence of conformity with best practice and of a risk management strategy. They are not, nor do they form part of, a governance framework. They are tools evidencing the application of governance principles.

In outsourcing its IT function, the case for an organisation to adopt corporate, IT and project governance principles is compelling, given the high incidence of project failure due to poor governance. It is not easy to embrace governance principles without the appropriate governance tools.

Familiarity with governance tools will provide the organisation with a distinct advantage in assessing the suitability of potential suppliers in the tendering process.

Governance structures

It is difficult to be definitive over the composition of a governance framework. Every organisation is different and, in the case of outsourcing, every project is different.

Senior management

However, common ground between the various models suggests that in respect of any IT services project, an organisation's governance structure starts with:

- the board of directors which sets the strategy and provides sponsorship for the project;
- a strategic steering committee, comprising a number of directors and key senior executives to oversee all of the organisation's projects, including an outsourcing project;
- an executive committee which assumes responsibility for the project, driving it forward, establishing lines of responsibility and accountability and delegating according to skills and capabilities.

Project management

The generic name given to the range of committees, or teams, involved in the management of an outsourcing project is 'procurement'. At the core of the procurement process is the project management team.

With involvement of the board and senior management committees as appropriate, the project management team might address, for instance: supplier tendering and selection; negotiations; the contract; and SLA – in fact, all steps up to and including the signature of the contract. Central to the project management team may be one

1: A Governance Overview

member concerned with contract issues; a second member concerned with commercial issues; and a third member concerned with operational issues.

Depending on the nature of the project, the project management team may wish to co-opt specialist assistance, either in house, or from external consultants.

Specialist teams

Some functions may require specialist members on the project management team or, subject to their complexity, separate teams of specialists, for example:

- IT: where the complexity and sophistication of IT to be outsourced requires specialist knowledge;
- asset management: where significant assets are to be transferred;
- human resources: where significant numbers of personnel are to be transferred;
- transition: where significant operational disruption is likely.

Teams operating within this general structure are subordinate and accountable to the project management team which, in turn, is responsible for defining their brief.

Risk and compliance

Two further functions underpin the entire structure:

- risk management: responsibility for general areas of strategic and operational risk arising during the project;

- compliance: responsibility for ensuring that all aspects of the project comply with current legal, regulatory and codified provisions, including information security.

These functions concern issues of strategy and should be managed at steering committee level. Risk and compliance are issues for the board. In the case of compliance, the organisation may not possess an adequate level of in-house expertise, in which case, access to external legal resources will be required.

Depending on the size of the organisation and the complexity of the project, it may not be necessary to constitute dedicated teams for the purposes of compliance or risk management. The important point is that the organisation recognises that compliance and risk management issues thread throughout and well beyond the management of the contracting process; and there must be prompt and reliable expertise available at short notice.

Exit committee

Once the contract expires, the organisation will need to consider whether to continue with the project under a new contract with updated provisions, or to bring some or all of the outsourced services in house.

If the organisation decides to bring the outsourced functions in house, it will need to re-constitute the IT function. The effort may be both complex and considerable. Much will depend on the extent and complexity of the original project, but bringing the outsourced function in house may be as involved as managing the original outsourcing project, if not more so.

1: A Governance Overview

An exit committee should manage contract termination procedures. The exit strategy will be the board's responsibility because the strategy must be aligned with the organisation's goals and objectives. The strategy will be driven by a board steering committee to which the exit committee will be responsible for implementation.

However difficult, and distant, it may be, the potential complexity of an exit strategy means the organisation should give as much consideration as possible to its exit strategy during the preliminary negotiations at the outset of the outsourcing project. This will enable the board to focus on potential complexities in the contract and how they can be managed.

Retained IT department

Once the contract is operative, the retained IT department assumes responsibility for a number of functions. The role performed by the retained IT department is an important factor in determining the success of the project.

The retained IT department has three roles. First, it must protect the organisation's interests under the contract and SLA. Examples include, for instance, contract management, finance management, performance management (including audits) and relationship management.

Second, it must maintain a 'partnership-style' interface with the supplier, ensuring that the supplier is aware of the organisation's needs and that issues and disputes are managed promptly and efficiently, and do not fester.

Third, it must manage the organisation's end-users, opening channels of communication, so that the organisation is aware of their changing needs and can proactively identify opportunities for innovation and competitive performance in the marketplace.

From a governance perspective, effective performance of this role is critical to the project's success. Within an IT governance framework, the retained IT department will be supervised, monitored and resourced, so that the supply chains from end-user to organisation to supplier, and from supplier to organisation to end-user remain robust, yet sufficiently flexible to meet changes in the business environment.

Even where the supplier offers contract management services, the retained IT department will need to ensure that the organisation is not outsourcing areas that are capable of in-house delivery and so incurring unnecessary expense.

More radically, the function moves away from performance management and more towards performance audit. Even if a supplier employs an independent auditor for its services, a potential conflict between auditor and supplier may arise in the case of an unfavourable report and the retained IT department may, therefore, wish to conduct its own audit.

Managing the supplier relationship

Successful management of the supplier relationship can be a challenge over a period of several years. Organisations and suppliers change; personnel change; business environments change. Relationships tend to be most successful when they are open and transparent, with adequate lines of communication – three important corporate governance principles. They facilitate a mutual understanding and appreciation of the parties' objectives.

1: A Governance Overview

It is preferable that the structures of both organisation and supplier should mirror each other. In other words, there should be corresponding executive, management and operational functions in each organisation able to communicate with each other on the same level.

Examples of where this is beneficial are: management of the contract and SLA; dispute escalation; and discussions over potential innovation. It is important that those involved in the project both within the organisation and the supplier, should, as far as possible, have respective counterparts with whom they can discuss problems and develop new ideas.

The organisation should satisfy itself that the supplier is culturally aligned with its business objectives. An organisation which has business objectives seeking safe and steady growth may have difficulty in developing a successful relationship with a highly entrepreneurial supplier intent on the rapid development of experimental solutions.

The seeds of a successful relationship are sown in the pre-contract phase, when the organisation must sift out potential difficulties and question critically the supplier's ability to meet its needs for quality services in the long term.

The organisation should establish any standards with which the supplier is certified, and any methodologies the supplier adopts. Data protection issues abound throughout any outsourcing project. An organisation might check, for instance, for certification under BS 10012:2009. A checklist of potential methodologies and standards should form part of the tendering and due diligence.

Ideally, in any governance structure, a supplier should match its application of governance principles and use of

1: A Governance Overview

governance tools with those of the organisation. A mutually sound understanding of governance offers an organisation a far greater prospect of successfully establishing at the outset whether a potential supplier will meet its objectives.

Cloud computing

Cloud computing has emerged as a radically different outsourcing model. Otherwise known as 'software-as-a-service' (SaaS), this is a web-based hosting service. Its key features are that it is subscriber-based, universally available and scalable for single (dedicated) or multiple organisations (multi-tenants). It is characterised by a less formal approach than the traditional outsourcing project.

The model is essentially that of utility computing because an essential feature is its provision as an 'on-demand' service, in the same way as domestic utilities, such as gas, water and electricity.

Cloud services are frequently provided from farms of virtualised servers each capable of holding vast amounts of data and serving multiple tenants. Although the services supplied in this model are usually commoditised and offered for a mass-market of multiple tenants, they can also be provided as a dedicated service for individual organisations.

The marked difference between the traditional model and the Cloud model lies in the relationship between the parties. The traditional model is based on a carefully negotiated and settled contract and SLA (usually drafted by the organisation), underpinned by extensive due diligence

1: A Governance Overview

processes and implemented by various layers of board, executive and operational management.

The Cloud model is more perfunctory. The contract and SLA are most commonly issued as standard by the supplier, almost on a 'take-it-or-leave-it', non-negotiable approach – just as in the case of a domestic utility service. The 'utility' approach has much less procedural formality than the traditional approach and is perceived as a much quicker and less cumbersome service.

The effect is to change the dynamics of the relationship. In the traditional model, the service is based on, and tailored to, the requirements of the organisation. While this remains the case to a larger extent in dedicated Cloud computing projects, in the multi-tenant model, the emphasis shifts to availability of the service. It is the service that is being sold, not the IT.

This is not necessarily a concern for an organisation. After all, domestic utilities are not provided on a tailored basis. However, an organisation in a multi-tenant environment may not be comfortable with this apparent loss of control.

Cloud computing is widely regarded as disruptive technology because of its ability to transform the IT services market. It can be available on an infrastructure, platform and application basis to mass markets. This has the potential to impact dramatically both on the current model of in-house IT services, and also on hosting suppliers providing dedicated services direct to organisations, because the Cloud model has the effect of by-passing the stages involved in these models.

One issue that is emerging is the potential complexity of the model. The variety, type and number of services capable of

1: A Governance Overview

delivery in the Cloud model pose a significant management problem. They promise to proliferate faster than the ability of Cloud consumers to manage them. An organisation might adopt the single tenant model for one set of services and a multi-tenant model for several other services. How is that to be co-ordinated in an organised way?

Gartner[1] has suggested the creation of Cloud brokerages to govern the use, performance and delivery of these types of service, to enhance service delivery and value.

Research director, Frank Kenny, explains:

... the future of cloud computing will be permeated with the notion of brokers negotiating relationships with providers of cloud services and the service customers. In this context, a broker might be software, appliances, platforms or suites of technologies that enhance the base services available through the cloud. Enhancement will include managing access to these services, providing greater security or even creating completely new services.[2]

Gartner divides the brokerage model into three categories:

- Cloud service intermediation: a service that enhances and adds value to multiple services, such as identity management or access management and where the broker may reside at the supplier's location; or at the organisation's location; or exist as a separate Cloud service.

---

[1] *Three Types of Cloud Brokerages Will Enhance Cloud Services*, Plummer DC & Kenny LF, Gartner, 11 May 2009.
[2] *Gartner Says Cloud Consumers Need Brokerages to Unlock the Potential of Cloud Services*, Gartner Press Release, 9 July 2009, available at: *www.gartner.com/it/page.jsp?id=1064712*. Permission to reproduce granted by Gartner.

1: A Governance Overview

- Aggregation: a service that combines multiple services into one or more new services to ensure data is modelled across all components services and integration and the movement and security of data between the organisation and the supplier.
- Cloud service arbitrage: a service similar to aggregation but allowing more flexibility and choice, for example providing multiple e-mail services through one service provider.

Yet for all the excitement surrounding the Cloud model, a recent survey by Gartner[3] has revealed that many organisations are 'underwhelmed' by their experiences and believe that SaaS is not the anticipated panacea.

The survey was conducted in 333 organisations in the US and UK. Respondents who had considered using SaaS, but had decided not to, were asked what factors they considered in making their decision. The findings are as follows:

- 42% cited high cost of service;
- 38% cited difficulty with integration; and
- 33% said the solution did not meet technical requirements.

Twiggy Lo, principal research analyst at Gartner, says that these issues must be addressed and resolved and that:

SaaS vendors must focus on truly delivering lower TCO, facilitating easier deployments that negate the need for expensive consulting support and providing more robust integration strategies that recognise the heterogeneous environments that most customers now run and will run in the

---

[3] *Dataquest Insight: SaaS Adoption Trends in the US and UK*, Pring B & Lo T, Gartner, 29 May 2009.

1: A Governance Overview

near future. Most importantly, vendors must reaffirm the fundamentals of the SaaS model – that SaaS solutions are lighter, more intuitive, more agile and more modest.[4]

Some key risks arise from Cloud computing. Principally, they revolve around the management, confidentiality and security of data. The storage of vast amounts of data in server farms presents the potential for data leakage, contamination and interference.

Equally problematic is the location of data. The DPA contains strict provisions governing the transfer of data internationally. With globally located server farms, how can an organisation be sure of: its location; the competence of its management; its protection from interference; its confidentiality; its security; the ability to secure access to it; its safe return; and the competence of the supplier in the whole operation?

Another concern is performance reliability and standards – unscheduled downtime or unexpected faults in the supplier's systems might result in significant loss to the organisation.

With the organisation operating in an environment in which the supplier has control, the reputation of the supplier is another critical issue.

As part of the Cloud model, suppliers are emerging who bundle or embed security within Cloud services, but the immaturity of the market and the absence of recognised

---

[4] *Gartner Survey Shows Many Users are Underwhelmed by Their Experiences of SaaS,* Gartner Press Release, 8 July 2009, available at: *www.gartner.com/it/page.jsp?id=1062512*. Permission to reproduce granted by Gartner.

1: A Governance Overview

benchmark certification to address Cloud services, mean that the nature and extent of the risks are a deterrent to wide market adoption. This makes the adoption of governance principles all the more compelling.

The less formal Cloud model still raises issues needing the application of governance principles. Examples include:

- supplier selection and due diligence procedures;
- ensuring the IT services offered meet its objectives;
- conditions governing transfer of data and other intellectual property;
- standards of service performance and delivery;
- the impact of operational disruption; and
- the impact on personnel arising from redeployment, redundancy and potential further recruitment.

The obligation of the board to apply governance principles in the adoption of Cloud services as a strategy remains equally valid for the traditional model. The principles of transparent decision making, clear lines of responsibility and accountability, risk and compliance management and realising stakeholder value, all apply to any Cloud project.

Similarly, IT governance principles – ensuring IT operates to support and achieve the organisation's objectives – are equally applicable.

The securing of IT services based on the Cloud model should be managed in the same way as a traditional outsourcing project. The organisation must ensure that adoption of Cloud services is part of a balanced portfolio of in-house and outsourced services and will supply an adequate return on investment. Although a simple concept, the Cloud model has the potential to develop into a complex range of services. Some organisations may decide

1: A Governance Overview

to 'mix and match' their portfolio of services, outsourcing more complex, tailored services through a traditional supplier, while entrusting more commoditised services, such as e-mail, to a Cloud provider. Others may opt for a combination of dedicated single tenant services and multi-tenant services – and even combine them with traditional services. Project governance principles still apply.

Complex risk and compliance issues proliferate, and are currently without any obvious solutions. They require management in the same way as in the traditional model.

Governance structures

How relevant and appropriate to the Cloud model is the governance structure suggested for the traditional model?

Board of directors

The decision to outsource an IT function to the Cloud environment, whether through a single-tenant, or multi-tenant model is a strategic decision to be made by the board. It involves the future direction of the organisation's IT strategy and may have significant implications for certain employees as well as financial, management and competitive considerations.

Steering and executive committees

For a straightforward project, an executive team may suffice, but for a complex 'mix and match' project both steering and executive teams may be needed, the former to ensure that the project integrates with the organisation's

1: A Governance Overview

existing IT infrastructure, the latter to drive the project forward.

Project management

Where the project is based on the dedicated single tenant model, the project team will have similar functions to those in the traditional model, because it will be the project management team's function to ensure the services are provided to the organisation's specification and requirements. This may involve more complexity surrounding supplier selection, tendering, negotiations, the contract and the SLA.

Where the project is based on the commoditised multi-tenant model, there will be less need for attention to such matters as, in a commoditised model, the processes are relatively standardised, although there will remain ongoing implementation issues to address.

Specialist teams

The requirement for expertise, in the areas of IT, asset management, human resources and transition will depend upon the range and complexity of services to be supplied.

For instance, if in adopting either the single tenant or multi-tenant model, there are issues concerning the transfer of assets or impacting on the position of employees, for instance, redundancies, some expertise may be required. The extent of the need for formal transition management will also depend on the impact of the project. Managing relatively minor impact could be part of the brief of the project team. Major impact, such as mass redundancies, would need formal transition management.

Risk and compliance

At the earliest stage and throughout the project, all levels of management should have available sufficient expertise in the areas of risk management and legal and regulatory compliance, including information security. The vehicle for providing this will depend on the range and complexity of the project. A relatively simple single tenant project may require only a risk manager, or external risk consultant, on the project management team, with compliance issues being outsourced to legal advisers.

In complex, multi-tenant projects, the organisation would be well-advised to have a breadth of expertise available with a sound understanding of the technological (including information security) and legal issues surrounding data management. This could comprise a combined risk and compliance team because in the Cloud model, the two are intertwined.

Retained IT department

In the Cloud model, the role of the retained IT department will depend on the model. In a dedicated single tenant model, the functions remain the same as, but may be less labour intensive than, the traditional model.

In the multi-tenanted, commoditised model, the functions will be less focused on maintaining the relationship as the services will be automated and commoditised, in the same

1: A Governance Overview

way as a consumer does not have a 'relationship' with a domestic utility provider.

In this model, the emphasis will be on demand management, ensuring that the contracted services are supplied as required, so that end-users' interests and expectations are met.

Conclusion

The adoption of an outsourcing strategy, whether traditional or Cloud, rests with the board. It should be made with governance principles uppermost in mind and applied to decision-making at every stage of the process.

Boards of directors embarking on outsourcing projects without the application of governance principles from the outset, as we shall see, face hazardous risks and challenging vulnerabilities that all too often are inadequately managed and can lead to project failure.

CHAPTER 2: THE IN-HOUSE IT CHALLENGE

The strategic outsourcing of IT systems is playing an increasingly significant, if not pivotal, role in the supply and delivery of goods and services.

A successful IT outsourcing process can revolutionise the performance of an organisation, increasing both its own profitability and the investment returns of its shareholders; as well as enhancing customer satisfaction and developing customer loyalty. There are clear benefits, for both the organisation and supplier, offered by outsourced IT services which are supplied efficiently and cost-effectively.

The legal sector is not always noted for its path-finding approach to the use of IT; however, lawyers are beginning to recognise the importance of strategic IT outsourcing.

In October 2006, one major law firm announced its intention to outsource much of its back-office (IT) to India in the expectation of making savings of almost £10 million on an annual basis.

Why is the outsourcing of IT systems and services becoming increasingly popular as an alternative strategy? Why should any organisation decide to offer the management of such a fundamental function to another organisation with which it may have no other common connection?

In recent years, the all-pervasive nature of information technology has helped spawn a global economy. Competition for business has moved from a market which was primarily domestic to a market in which many organisations now contend with world-wide competitors.

2: The In-house IT Challenge

In order to meet this competition successfully, organisations need to be both suitably structured and managed to the highest possible standards. Because global competition is so diffuse and is encouraged to operate to best practice standards, organisations need to equip themselves with strategies that will enable them to compete on an even playing field.

An organisation that has opted for an IT outsourcing strategy will almost certainly have made a conscious decision that the structure and/or performance of its IT department cannot: perform adequately in the competitive environment in which the organisation is operating; or meet the needs of its customers sufficiently; or develop its market share sufficiently.

The traditional structure of an in-house IT department is usually characterised by certain features. The department is likely to be headed by an IT director, perhaps a chief technology officer (CTO), or a chief information officer (CIO) answerable to a board of directors, beneath whom there will be layers of management comprising executive personnel, and administrative and clerical staff, according to the extent of the role and function of the department.

The importance of IT

IT is vital to every organisation. Without IT facilities virtually no organisation could survive, let alone compete, in the fast-moving global marketplace. Without IT, an organisation could not administer a workforce, nor import and export goods and services, nor respond to fast-moving change in almost every market.

2: The In-house IT Challenge

Organisations depend on IT for mapping out the strategic future of their business and supporting the supply and demand functions of current business operations. All organisations have 'business systems' comprising their people, their business processes, their business infrastructures and, underpinning these components, their IT.

IT offers support for specific business applications required to meet customer demand, for instance, online payment facilities and general business applications, such as the availability of e-mail and other messaging systems. IT is fundamental to the operations of every organisation. When IT systems fail, almost every other aspect of the business is affected. When IT systems fail to produce the required results, the profitability, and even the survival of the business is put at risk.

Not only is IT an enabling resource for the effective performance of the organisation, it is also a tool whereby an organisation can respond to change with suitable agility. Increasingly sophisticated developments in IT, such as Cloud computing, result in the emergence of new business models and increasingly efficient and cost-effective ways of performing.

In short, the modern organisation no longer operates in a settled and predictable environment. The risk for the modern organisation in a fast-moving global market is not only that it operates without adequate IT systems; but also that the IT systems with which it is equipped soon become legacy systems and the organisation suddenly finds itself ill-equipped to compete effectively.

It is against this backdrop that an organisation looks to the outsourcing of its IT function to specialist suppliers able to provide the economy, the agility and the necessary standard of performance that enables the organisation to compete on a level playing field.

IT functions

The purpose of the in-house IT department is to provide an IT function that enables the organisation to achieve business objectives; a function that aligns itself with the strategic plan of the organisation. Very broadly, this involves:

- the acquisition, maintenance and upgrade of hardware and software required for the organisation's activities;
- the development, management, supervision and maintenance of the organisation's network;
- the assurance of business continuity and information security;
- applications for, and renewal of, software licences;
- management of the organisation's IT infrastructure – personal computers; servers, etc;
- provision of educating and training;
- compliance with applicable laws and regulations; and
- provision of the IT function within a budget approved by the board.

Function analysis

The functions of the in-house IT function can be broadly categorised as follows:

2: The In-house IT Challenge

Strategic

The overall strategic objective of the IT function is, through its link to the core business of the organisation, to align itself with the organisation's goals and deliver planned value. In order to achieve this effectively, the IT function must be sufficiently agile in its marketplace activity.

Managerial

The managerial structure is traditionally hierarchical with the CIO or CTO at the head of a pyramid, with layers of managerial, executive and administrative support, defined roles and a recruitment strategy to comply with this infrastructure.

Operational

The key operational requirements are: the assurance of both business continuity and information security; compliance with legal, regulatory, codified provisions relevant to the IT function; and conformity to trade, industry and best practice standards.

Financial

The key financial issues are:

- investment in training and education in IT skills;
- investment in hardware, software and infrastructure;
- the cost of legal and regulatory compliance;
- the cost of security;
- the delivery of value for the IT investment;
- acceptable and audited performance levels.

2: The In-house IT Challenge

Such a broad range of responsibilities requires an equally broad range of skills and capabilities. Assembling a stable team of individuals with such a variety of skills is not an easy task; nor is maintaining the team over a sustained period of time.

A brief analysis of these categories reveals that just some of the skills, knowledge and capabilities involve: an appreciation of the importance of strategic planning in line with business goals; performance measurement and an understanding of financial controls; managerial and administrative competence; recruitment; human resources and marketing abilities; an understanding of legal and compliance issues; and an appreciation of the values of codes of practice and industry standards.

At the same time, the IT team must operate with a performance characterised by a sure-footed, yet agile, approach that enables it to respond to directions from the board, often prompted by unforeseen and rapid changes in the marketplace. At a time when competition arises from infinite sources, this is a tall order.

Performance challenges

The traditional model of the in-house IT department is presented with a number of serious performance challenges, especially when confronted with a complex network of possibly several hundred users scattered over several different countries.

2: The In-house IT Challenge

Competition

In terms of competition, IT is an essential tool for maintaining competitive advantage. However, as an in-house function, it is resource-intensive and can be slow to respond to the needs of its end-users and to innovate dynamically in order to compete in the marketplace.

The global market exacerbates this situation. Enhanced information and knowledge-sharing on a global basis, the emergence of virtual technologies, and the myriad legislative and regulatory provisions applicable in different jurisdictions simply add to the pressure on IT departments to perform.

Specialisms and niche markets

As the IT marketplace becomes increasingly sophisticated in response to customer demand for specialist solutions to address complex problems, the IT department has to expand its range of skills and competencies.

At the same time, it must also ensure that its function remains aligned with the core business skills of the organisation. This can present distracting problems if the niche market offers considerable business potential.

Economies of scale

At the other end of the spectrum, where customer demand arises from the volume-provider sector, the IT department has a similar issue to address. To what extent is it capable of adjusting its function from, say, a specialist provider, to a niche market when confronted with an attractive proposition that requires a 'mass market' solution?

2: The In-house IT Challenge

In each case, the organisation will need to review the strategic, managerial, operational and financial skills and capabilities of its IT function.

Cost

The overheads involved in managing and operating IT systems and IT networks are significant. After the human resources budget, the IT budget is likely to be highest. It is often thought that, as they develop, IT systems and networks become less expensive to acquire and deploy.

However, major business changes, increased and more sophisticated customer demands, technological developments, political and compliance changes all contradict this. It is no longer appropriate to consider IT aspects in isolation. The whole picture must be considered, so that important cost implications are not overlooked.

Compliance

A key issue facing any organisation running its own IT department is the requirement for compliance with the numerous legislative and regulatory provisions that now govern almost every aspect of the IT function. They range from the Health & Safety (Display Screen Equipment) Regulations 1992 to the Sarbanes-Oxley Act 2002.

Not only do civil and criminal sanctions arise from non-compliance; there is also the cost of compliance, for instance, the employment of staff to ensure compliance with the DPA or to check compliance with applicable foreign laws.

2: The In-house IT Challenge

Whether the cost of compliance assurance arises from recruitment of in-house personnel or periodic referrals to external consultants, the result is the same – an increased burden of responsibility and additional cost of providing the IT function.

Culture

If the IT function is to perform to the standards required by the organisation so as to enhance the prospects of the organisation in pursuit of its business goals, a culture that embraces IT is essential.

Lack of an IT culture is often characterised by reluctance to incur capital expenditure or an intolerant attitude to technology often endemic among organisations. The consequent lack of skill and senior management commitment to IT leaves organisations with inadequate systems and ill-equipped personnel. When IT departments lack the skills to provide cost-effective systems, the result is expensive technology which is barely of any practical use.

Embedding this culture can be a formidable challenge, especially without board-level commitment. There may be expertise at board-level in respect of strategic, managerial, operational and financial functions of IT identified earlier – but it is unlikely. It is difficult to embed a culture of enthusiasm for a business function where, at top level, there is inadequate experience and expertise, or simply downright ignorance.

2: The In-house IT Challenge

Conclusion

Significant challenges face IT departments structured on the in-house model. That is not to say that the traditional model is either obsolete or wholly incapable of performing to maximum efficiency. However, in the context of ensuring that the IT function performs to maximum effect, there are clearly significant tensions.

The most obvious is the wide range of responsibilities that now confronts the traditional IT department. The sheer volume and complexity of issues requires a detailed assessment of risk supported by an effective risk control strategy.

Recruitment and retention of a settled team of the required calibre is critical. A team that continually changes tends not to perform well. Retention of highly skilled and qualified personnel involves adroit management and, inevitably, a financial commitment to match.

At a time of economic recession, boards of directors scrutinise IT budgets critically and frequently conjure up reasons for a reduction.

Unsurprisingly, in response to this dilemma, many organisations are finding that an outsourced IT strategy is an alternative well worth exploration.

CHAPTER 3: OUTSOURCING CONSIDERATIONS

Definition

IT outsourcing involves an organisation contracting out services to a supplier to be performed to agreed levels over a set period of time. Sometimes, it includes one or more of the organisation's personnel, IT assets and premises being transfer to the supplier.

Outsourcing should not be confused with other expressions often used when referring to the function. Terms, such as association, arrangement or partnership, are sometimes loosely used to describe the outsourcing process. None correctly reflects the formal relationship involved in an outsourcing project.

An outsourced project creates a formal legal relationship between organisation and supplier which is governed by a contract and supported by an SLA and any other documents required to reflect the parties' respective rights and obligations.

Partnerships, in particular, are recognised in law as involving a joint sharing of benefits, risks and responsibilities. The outsourcing relationship is created at arm's length and while benefits and risks arise, they are not shared jointly. Similarly, 'arrangement' and 'association' are terms that are too vague to reflect accurately the close legal definition of the positions of both customer and supplier bound by contract.

3: Outsourcing Considerations

Outsourcing trends

It is instructive to see the growing popularity of outsourcing IT functions.

According to analysts at Gartner, the SaaS enterprise applications markets will more than double by 2012 to $14.8 billion, after a strong demand in 2008. Worldwide SaaS revenue in the ... market is set to surpass $6.4 billion in 2008, a 27% annual rise.

'The popularity of the on-demand deployment model has increased significantly within the last four years. Initial concerns over security, response time, and service availability have diminished for many organisations as SaaS business and computing models have matured and adoption has become pervasive,' says Sharon Mertz, a research director at Gartner.[5]

Other sources claim that outsourcing will continue to grow over the next five years and will include a wide variety of both core and support IT applications across commercial enterprises.

IT outsourcing has gained considerable popularity which, it seems, will only continue to increase. If a significant number of competitors are outsourcing their IT functions, it is surely essential for an organisation to investigate this in order to maintain and increase its competitive advantage.

General considerations

Making the business case for outsourcing an IT function requires careful consideration. Approaching such a project is far more complex than simply making a decision in the

---

[5] *Software as a service demand growing,* Robinson J, *www.information-age.com,* 19 November 2008.

3: Outsourcing Considerations

hope and expectation that complete responsibility for IT is abdicated to an independent third party.

Underpinning the decision to outsource must be the ability to show that this is in line with the goals of the business and supports a viable business case. This is a fundamental requirement to the decision and is the context in which any decision to outsource must be reached.

An organisation might base its business case on its IT mission statement, citing: the need for innovative IT; the need for a timely and efficient response to its customer's needs; the desire to provide a proactive, quality service; the requirement for a reliable IT infrastructure; and the determination to offer a service of excellence.

The organisation must ask itself some critical questions in the decision-making process. These considerations must be debated at board level. The decision to outsource an IT function is a strategic issue; how the project is undertaken is an operational issue, although there may be strategic questions that arise from the management of the project.

The board should address the strategic issues which involve an overview of the intended project. In the context of the need to align the purpose of the project with business goals, typical strategic questions include:

- How does the proposed project fit in with the overall business objectives of the organisation?
- Is the decision to outsource being taken at the correct stage in terms of the strategic (and possibly operational) business plans of the organisation?
- What are the financial implications of a decision to proceed with the project (for instance, would it be an

equally cost-effective strategy to acquire in-house skills)?
- What are the managerial and organisational implications of a decision to outsource (for example, human resource changes)?
- What are the intended strategic benefits for the organisation and are they realistic (for example, to address competition in a specialist area)?
- What potential might there be for the supplier to develop solutions in order to attract business in a niche area that complements the business plan?

Each organisation will have different considerations; but, at a strategic level, uppermost in a board's mind must be that the outsourcing strategy must be consistent with, and subordinate to, the overall strategic plan of the business.

If the decision to outsource is strategically viable, operational issues then need consideration. These may be considered at board level but must necessarily involve managerial expertise because it is management that oversees the implementation of projects. Each organisation has individual concerns, but typical issues to consider include:

- What provisions must there be to safeguard the security of the organisation's data?
- What are the risks of confidentiality being compromised during or after completion of the project?
- What steps can be taken to measure the quality of the supplier's performance?
- How can the supplier's use of systems and software be controlled, or exploited, for maximum benefit to the organisation?

3: Outsourcing Considerations

- What is the potential for personality conflicts arising between the respective management functions of the customer and supplier?

Frequently, strategic and operational issues are confused. Important strategic issues may be subordinated to more trivial operational issues as a result of which a decision is not truly based on the business case. At board level, it is vital that a debate on strategic issues is not hijacked by those with particular interest in more functional operational considerations.

IT considerations

The strategic and operational issues considered could apply both to an in-house IT project as well as an IT outsourcing project. However, an IT outsourcing project involves particular considerations. It is helpful to consider these in five categories: strategy, technology, compliance, operations and finance.

Underlying all these considerations is the principle that information and related technology now play a critical role in determining the ability of an organisation to compete in the global marketplace.

Strategy

The need to ensure that the organisation's use of IT enhances its competitiveness will be a dominant motivating factor behind any decision to outsource. At the earliest possible stage, it must be considered whether it is viable to acquire the necessary skills in house, or to outsource all, or part, of the IT function.

3: Outsourcing Considerations

Much will depend on the extent to which the IT function is a core competence of the organisation. There are two primary considerations. Can outsourcing improve the organisation's performance of its core activity? Will outsourcing core IT functions significantly affect the organisation's name and trading activities in the marketplace?

Factors in assessing whether an activity is a core competence include: whether the IT function is capable of imitation; the range of experience and knowledge within the organisation; and the ability to access a wide variety of markets through its IT function.

In-house IT functions that are core to an organisation's strategic plan will be viewed less favourably for an outsourcing project than IT functions that are peripheral or common in many other organisations, because loss of core competence is likely to reduce the organisation's ability to compete and may lead it to a position of over-dependency on the supplier.

So fundamental is the need for an effective IT function, that an error in understanding the implications of outsourcing IT could result in a significant loss of strategic agility or flexibility. The board must decide whether the organisation will remain more responsive to customer needs by retaining control of the function in house, and perhaps having to acquire new skills, or whether a more experienced or better equipped supplier might be more successful. The critical issue is to identify the IT strategy which will best meet the organisation's business goals.

None of these considerations can be met adequately, unless there is commitment at board level to the decision to outsource the IT function. While many business leaders

3: Outsourcing Considerations

accept that IT is vital for achieving the organisation's strategic goals, there is frequently widespread ignorance or misunderstanding of how IT actually performs.

It is widely recognised that interest and commitment to IT strategies and functions at board level are variable. An ill-informed and indifferent approach to outsourcing the IT function is likely to result in a decision that fails to take adequate account of the strategic implications.

Technology

From a technology perspective, the concerns of the board may be that, by opting for outsourcing the IT function, a degree of control is being sacrificed. However, that is not necessarily the case.

By outsourcing an IT function, the board is not losing control of its IT strategy. It is the day-to-day management and operation of systems and software required to meet its needs that is being passed to the supplier. Further, as will be seen, this 'delegation' is underpinned by a contract and supported by an SLA under which the performance of the supplier is monitored.

The board will need to ensure that a decision to outsource will not result in any reduction in the quality and efficiency of the IT function; in other words, that the supplier will provide a better managed, more cost-effective IT function of equal, if not better, quality and performance.

Linked to this is the need for the capability of the supplier to provide the type of service required by the organisation's customers. The supplier must be able to offer either niche, or volume, services according to the organisation's needs. The objective of outsourcing the IT function is that the

3: Outsourcing Considerations

supplier has IT skills, competence and systems that the organisation either does not possess, or for which it is unable to make, or cannot make, a business case for their acquisition.

Two further technology issues require consideration. An assurance of business continuity is essential. While legal responsibilities between the parties will be governed by a contract and SLA, it is the IT and business context that will equally concern the board. Measures must be taken to ensure that the supplier possesses adequate back-up IT and effective policies in procedures.

The potential for innovative IT solutions is another factor. An agile response by an IT function is critical to successful competition. If the organisation's customers require imaginative IT solutions, the supplier must be equipped to meet these demands, otherwise the organisation will derive insufficient benefit from the project.

Compliance

Legal, regulatory and compliance requirements are major issues for organisations and significant drivers for more effectively managed IT functions. In contemplating an IT outsourcing strategy, compliance is a vital consideration.

In the context of midsize organisations, according to Gartner[6]:

---

[6] *Best practices for midsize businesses seeking cost-effective compliance*, Gartner RAS Core Research Note: G00162997, November 2008.

3: Outsourcing Considerations

... midsize businesses face unique challenges in addressing complex, multifaceted compliance requirements. Security managers and other professionals with compliance responsibilities for midsize companies need to move beyond the tactical 'one-off' compliance projects and take a comprehensive, strategic approach to this critical function.

Key findings included:

- Midsize businesses often approach compliance as a 'necessary evil' attempting to make the minimum effort necessary to meet regulatory requirements.
- In the absence of a formal information governance programme, tactical concerns can make the cost-effective execution of compliance strategy difficult for resource-constrained businesses.
- Failure to achieve the level of compliance required by management's risk-profile preferences may jeopardise shareholder value and reputation, but exceeding that level may cost more than is justified.

These observations apply to all organisations regardless of size.

In terms of outsourcing IT, most publicity surrounds issues of confidentiality and security of data. Underlying data compliance is the need for an organisation to protect its intellectual property. This is of particular importance in an IT outsourcing strategy where large amounts of an organisation's data may be placed under the management of the supplier.

Intellectual property, sometimes known as intellectual capital, comprises assets that are not necessarily measurable but which benefit an organisation. This will include, for instance, skilled personnel, customer goodwill, patents, collaborators, stakeholders and reputation.

Legal and regulatory issues are considered later. For the present, a brief sweep of the range of compliance provisions gives an idea of the task. Relevant to IT outsourcing may be legal provisions governing: product liability; misleading advertisements; conformance with quality standards; environmental regulations; and health and safety regulations.

In addition, there are provisions governing specialist areas, such as Sarbanes Oxley and codes of practice issued by the FSA. Legal and regulatory compliance can be overwhelmingly burdensome in terms of management and cost.

Operations

Operational issues concern the mechanics of the organisation – the business systems and procedures through which it executes its business plan, to meet customer needs, provide adequate remuneration for directors and employees and provide a satisfactory return to its stakeholders.

The key operational functions are an organisation's IT function and its HR functions. Understanding the HR implications is critical to approaching outsourcing successfully.

Whether the organisation's IT function alone (excluding personnel) is to be outsourced, or whether the organisation is to outsource the whole function, including HR, there will be significant implications.

If the former arrangement is intended, the organisation will be left with a potentially redundant team of personnel with whom compensation packages must be agreed, if no other acceptable role can be provided.

3: Outsourcing Considerations

If the latter arrangement is intended, the organisation must comply with employment protection provisions. The organisation will also need to address the question of recruiting personnel with relevant managerial skills and qualifications so as to oversee the outsourcing project and ensure its smooth operation. This will certainly involve relationship management skills as the respective responsibilities of organisation and supplier require attention.

Finance

The availability of only limited resources is a critical factor for any organisation, especially so in an economic downturn.

The impact of strategic, technology, compliance and operational considerations inevitably has cost implications. It is critically important that the organisation has access, whether internally or externally, to sufficient expertise in respect of detailed financial information to enable an accurate assessment to be made of the total financial commitment.

Important financial aspects to be considered include:

- the total cost of the time engaged on the project by (senior) personnel in the organisation;
- the cost of access to consultancy services before, during and after the project;
- the cost of access to legal services before, during and after the project;
- the cost of securing licences for the use of any software by the supplier in the outsourcing process;
- the cost of compensating any redundant personnel;

3: Outsourcing Considerations

- the cost of any employment protection payments in respect of transferred staff;
- the cost of recruiting additional personnel to manage the contract and SLA;
- the supplier's charges under the contract; and
- hidden costs, for example, where the supplier imposes charges for services mistakenly assumed to be covered.

As every organisation and every outsourcing project is different, there may be other specific cost considerations to be taken into account. Expenditure, such as salary and general overheads can be calculated, but outsourcing may involve 'surprise' expenditure, such as the cost of processing and supplier charges which are not always recognised and considered at the outset. With respect to this expenditure, the organisation must ensure that the project is justified by the anticipated return on investment.

Objectives

The organisation must ensure that the IT outsourcing strategy is aligned with its business goals. This is best established by analysis of the organisation's objectives in adopting the strategy in the first instance.

If the objectives of the strategy are not considered in the decision-making process, there is likely to be confusion over the role and purpose of the strategy against the organisation's business plan. In that event, the project will be less effectively executed and will yield less than the anticipated return on investment.

Identifying and defining objectives shape the nature and key features of the project. Each organisation will have its own objectives. Some of the more typical include:

3: Outsourcing Considerations

- to decrease the overheads of maintaining the IT function;
- to obtain a greater return for the organisation's investment in the IT function;
- to embark on a programme of specialist IT innovation with a view to expanding into new markets;
- to eliminate the entire cost of maintaining the IT function;
- to enable the organisation to concentrate on its core business; or
- recognition that the organisation's IT function is essentially a mass-market operation and suitable for outsourcing.

The Outsourcing Institute[7] suggests the following reasons:

- reduction of operating costs;
- improvement of company focus;
- resources not available internally;
- free resources for other purposes; and
- access to world-class capabilities.

The objectives may be one or a mixture of any of these. Once objectives are understood and agreed, the organisation can shape the process of the project to meet its requirements.

For instance, the provisions of the outsourcing contract and the SLA where the objective is to eliminate the cost of the IT function will differ from those where the objective is to develop innovative software. In the latter case, the focus will fall on the performance of the supplier in developing

---

[7] *The Outsourcing Institute IT Index 2001*, Casale F, www.outsourcing.com.

3: Outsourcing Considerations

solutions that gain acceptance in new markets. In turn, this will influence the selection of the supplier.

Where the objective is intended to achieve a more economic performance, the emphasis may fall on the need for fixed costs and the avoidance of hidden or escalating expense.

Where return on investment is the priority, the contract will focus on the need for the supplier to adapt to changing markets while at the same time ensuring that the organisation is not subjected to unwarranted expense occasioned by operational changes.

In setting its objectives, the organisation will need to decide such issues as: the organisation's high-level objectives; its core competencies; its differentials in the marketplace; its customers' needs and its current capability of meeting them; the existing skills in the organisation; and its approach to developing new markets.

Stakeholders

No assessment of the objectives of outsourcing will be adequate without addressing stakeholders' interests.

The IT Governance Institute[8] explains:

> ... setting strategy, managing risks, allocating resources, delivering value and measuring performance, are the stakeholder values, which drive the enterprise and IT strategy.
>
> 'Stakeholder' indicates anyone who has either a responsibility for or an expectation from the enterprise's IT, e.g., shareholders,

---

[8] Source: www.itgi.org. ©2009 IT Governance Institute. All rights reserved. Used by permission.

3: Outsourcing Considerations

directors, executives, business and technology management, users, employees, governments, suppliers, customers and the public.

It is important to appreciate the different approach that each stakeholder will have towards the objective of an outsourcing project. The description above suggests a wide variety of different interests, some internal and others external to the organisation.

Stakeholder potential for helping or hindering the project is important and at an early stage it should be considered how stakeholders' interests will impact on the process and progress of the project.

A glance at the wide range of stakeholders in any organisation reveals many conflicting interests. Directors, shareholders, compliance officers, finance managers, project managers, employees and end-users all have differing individual agendas and personal objectives, although they are commonly bound by a single objective – the success of the project.

These diverse interests emphasise the need to plan an outsourcing project that is aligned to a formal business plan and intended to achieve its goals and only when these differing interests are properly understood can a shared agenda for the IT outsourcing strategy be created.

CHAPTER 4: REACHING THE DECISION

The challenges facing an in-house IT function were considered in the second chapter, followed by discussion of the business implications of adopting an IT outsourcing strategy from strategic, technology, compliance, operational and financial perspectives, including objectives and stakeholders' interests.

However, before a decision to outsource is reached, there must be a clear understanding of the potential advantages and disadvantages of outsourcing the IT function.

Advantages and disadvantages are often subjective. What may be advantageous for one organisation may be disadvantageous for another and will depend on an organisation's individual circumstances.

This chapter considers the potential advantages and disadvantages of the outsourcing environment from the perspective of the organisation proposing to outsource its IT to a supplier. The analysis is structured into strategic, technology, compliance, operational and financial categories.

Advantages

Strategy

- **Core competence:** this is the collective learning within the organisation – its know-how or intellectual property. An IT outsourcing strategy enables an organisation to focus and develop its activities around its core competence and to delegate ancillary and less profitable

activities to a supplier. In the case of the IT function, standard or mass-produced IT is often selected for outsourcing.
- **Competition:** the specialist skills and IT systems placed by the supplier at the organisation's disposal can offer the organisation a significant competitive advantage.
- **Defined objectives:** outsourcing the IT function to a specialist supplier enables well-defined objectives to be clearly identified – a major business consideration discussed in the previous chapter. These objectives will be identifiable in both the outsourcing contract and the SLA.
- **Major IT changes:** an outsourcing strategy may be adopted in order to bring about significant business change within an organisation, for instance, where an organisation decides to develop new niche services.

Technology

- **Expertise:** the selection of a suitable supplier offers the organisation an opportunity to take advantage of the IT skills and expertise of the supplier. This will enable the organisation to focus on offering enhanced products and services.
- **Innovation:** the same skills and expertise combined with access to more sophisticated systems will enable the organisation to develop initiatives and devise innovative IT solutions to meet customer needs. This offers the chance to compete for new business development opportunities.
- **IT changes:** the supplier will operate in a specialist market. Outsourcing the IT function enables the organisation to be more agile and responsive to customer

4: Reaching the Decision

needs that involve significant or frequent changes of hardware, software or systems.

Compliance

- **Certainty:** perhaps the most beneficial aspect of outsourcing from a compliance perspective is that, provided the contract and SLA adequately protect the organisation's interests, clarity and certainty is brought to bear on responsibility for compliance throughout the project.
- **Responsibilities:** the outsourcing contract and SLA will identify and define the legal and compliance obligations and responsibilities of the parties in support of the objectives of the project.
- **Performance:** the contract and the SLA will set benchmarks for the supplier's performance of the outsourcing project and will contain provisions governing the compensation to be paid for any breach of contract by the supplier.

Operations

- **Administration:** one of the least popular aspects of the in-house IT function is the administration surrounding its performance. Outsourcing removes this responsibility from the organisation. Under the contract and SLA, the supplier will assume responsibility for such issues as: maintenance of networks; management of systems; software upgrades; retention of data; and other management issues associated with the IT function.
- **IT personnel:** where the outsourcing contract includes provision for the outsourcing of IT personnel, there may

be a correspondingly reduced operational responsibility for the management of HR aspects of the IT function – and any accommodation occupied for the purpose
- **Reduction of workload:** the organisation's in-house IT-related workload will be reduced and its activities can be directed either to its core business or towards developing other activities.
- **Flexibility:** the availability of a specialist IT supplier should enable the organisation to respond to customer demand with more agility. In contrast with an internal IT department for which the acquisition of new hardware, software, IT infrastructure and skills may be required, a supplier of any repute will be acquainted with emerging trends and supply products and services that enable the organisation to respond to the needs of its customers.
- **Control:** as a managerial issue, the availability of a supplier, bound by, and accountable under, a contract to meet the requirements of the organisation offers control over the quality and standard of the outsourced services without the burden associated with managing an in-house department.

Finance

- **'Overhead' expenditure:** one of the immediate benefits to the organisation will be the absence of the overheads that managing an in-house IT function carries. While it is true that these may be included in the supplier's cost of providing the service, the sum will be defined in the SLA and will be more convenient for budgetary management.
- **Pricing:** the contract and SLA will define the pricing structure of the services to be provided. The certainty of

4: Reaching the Decision

the structure will help reduce the chances of the organisation being surprised by unexpected expenditure to finance the provision of services caused by customer demand.
- **Penalties:** the SLA will contain penalty clauses intended to ensure that the supplier provides the contracted services on time and to budget.
- **Audit:** the SLA will include provision for its auditors to check the supplier's performance against recognised auditing standards.

Disadvantages

Superficially, the case for an IT outsourcing strategy is attractive. The contract and SLA inject a measure of certainty over the relationship and the standards of performance of the agreed services. The supplier has the expertise and is able to take managerial, financial and operational responsibility for providing the service.

Many organisations see outsourcing as a chance to offload the financial and managerial commitment of the in-house IT function, especially where there is inadequate top-level commitment.

Many organisations find the offer of regular pricing mechanisms under an outsourcing contract, according to time or units of services consumed, to be tempting in the face of the 'peaks and troughs' of maintaining an in-house facility.

However, that approach is something of a simplification of the issue as the concerns below reveal.

4: Reaching the Decision

Strategy

- **Adverse strategic impact:** an in-house IT function, with its intimate knowledge of the organisation, should be better positioned to respond to the needs of the organisation's customers. The CIO or CTO can ensure first-hand that the IT function is performed in line with business goals and customer needs. Outsourcing the IT function may reduce this strategic control. The cost-benefit may be more difficult to assess or the supplier may prove unable to meet the organisation's demands.
- **Loss of control:** although an outsourcing function can provide a measure of control for the organisation, in some respects the reverse is true. If the organisation requires new services, the contract and SLA will need amendment. If performance levels are inadequate, the reputation of the organisation will be damaged. Although the contract and SLA provide certainty for the organisation, the very nature of a contract means that the organisation becomes dependent upon the supplier for its satisfactory performance.
- **Multi-sourcing:** if the needs of the organisation cannot be met by one supplier, more than one supplier may be required. This can present considerable strategic, managerial and administrative complexity. Challenges of multi-sourcing involve: managing a contract and SLA with each supplier and managing multi-supplier relationships which the original outsourcing strategy may not have contemplated. Managing contracts with multiple suppliers is discussed later.
- **Loss of core competence:** outsourcing the IT function, together with the organisation's dependency on the supplier, can lead to a position where the supplier assumes a dominance that reduces or removes the

4: Reaching the Decision

organisation's core skills, as a result of which the organisation risks surrendering its market to the supplier or even other competition.

Technology

- **Loss of skills:** the removal of the IT function, whether or not the outsourcing contract includes a transfer of personnel, will involve a loss of skill and expertise – the intellectual property or know-how – from within the organisation. If the entire IT function is outsourced, this may not directly affect the organisation's performance but there may remain insufficient expertise to oversee the performance of the supplier.
- **Lock-in:** in an outsourcing project, the organisation effectively becomes integrated with the supplier in that its IT skills and services are replaced by those of the supplier. This leveraging may result in poor performance and investment by an unscrupulous supplier and reduce the incentive to innovate. The organisation's dependency gives rise to a risk of the organisation becoming over-reliant, even 'locked-in' to the systems of the supplier.

Compliance

- **Data security:** outsourcing the IT function is likely to involve the supplier processing the organisation's data in some form. The organisation remains responsible for compliant handling of its data even if this is under the control of a supplier. Risks may arise over the confidentiality of the organisation's data and intellectual property. For instance, there may be misuse of confidential data relating to the organisation, its

employees and customers; and inadequate security measures implemented by the supplier.
- **Business continuity:** linked to the issue of security are the questions of business continuity and the danger of interruption to the supplier's service. Particular concerns include any effect on the organisation's performance which may affect customers or provide the competition with an advantage.
- **Employment legislation:** any transfer of personnel will require compliance with the relevant employment protection legislation, as will the issue of any redundancies that arise from the outsourcing process.
- **Supplier leveraging:** the issue of supplier-leveraging is an IT issue, but there are also compliance implications. If a supplier is able to assume a dominant position, the temptation may arise to be casual over compliance with the provisions of the contract and the SLA.

Operations

- **Impact on personnel:** the loss of personnel resulting from an outsourcing project can have an adverse impact on both the personnel in the transfer and those remaining with the organisation. The former may feel unsettled in working for a new employer, perhaps even more so if the transfer involves a change of premises. The latter may feel a sense of rejection or uncertainty which may affect their performance.
- **Cost of personnel:** the concept of outsourcing often carries with it the idea that it is a less expensive option than employing personnel in house. In fact, the human resource aspect of outsourcing can involve even higher overheads because of the supplier's need to recruit

personnel with a range of skills that will meet the requirements of its other 'customer' organisations. These overheads may be reflected in the supplier's charges.
- **Supplier leveraging:** leveraging can also impact on the performance of the outsourcing operation. The supplier may be tempted to minimise its costs by employing reduced numbers of personnel on the project or introduce other economies to reduce overall expenditure.

Finance

- **Increasing cost:** although the supplier's charges will be governed by the contract and SLA, the danger of escalating cost must be recognised. Outsourcing projects that last for a number of years, situations involving major changes to the organisation's requirements, or within the business environment often entail unforeseen increases in cost. Quite independently, there will be the cost of running a retained IT department to manage the contract and relationship with the supplier. This is considered in detail later.
- **Supplier dominance:** the supplier may leverage a superior business position by finding opportunities to increase costs and charges through amendments to the contract and SLA. The organisation should not forget that the supplier's primary motive is to generate as much profit as the project can generate.
- **New skills:** the need to manage the outsourcing project in an IT department retained by the organisation is likely to involve the organisation in recruiting new personnel with, for instance, skills in performance management and audit, in order to address any concerns over the supplier's performance under the contract and SLA.

4: Reaching the Decision

Offshore outsourcing

Offshore outsourcing is a subset of the organisation's overall decision to outsource. It is not a separate strategy although there will be additional considerations when arriving at the decision to outsource to an offshore destination. However, it is important to understand that any decision to outsource to an offshore destination must be taken in the context of the need for the strategy to be aligned with the business goals and objectives of the organisation.

India is one of the most popular offshore outsourcing destinations. IT solutions development and call-centres are frequently outsourced functions. While the usual objectives of reduced costs and the availability of a more skilled workforce are part of the business case, other issues, specific to offshore outsourcing, also arise. These include, for example: political and economic instability; differences of culture; language complications; insecure infrastructures; and risks to data confidentiality.

Legal issues

The outsourcing contract will govern the legal relationship between the parties, supported by an SLA reflecting performance standards to be achieved. Outsourcing contracts and supplemental agreements are considered later in detail. The majority of legal issues arise from the need to ensure the application of the correct law and jurisdiction in the case of an offshore outsourcing contract. Below are listed some of the principal considerations.

4: Reaching the Decision

Data

Provisions to ensure that data remains secure and confidential are implemented in the UK by the DPA. This is considered later in more detail. However, special provisions govern the export of data to international destinations. The organisation will need assurance that similar provisions governing the security and confidentiality of data apply in the intended offshore destination.

Intellectual property

The law relating to intellectual property may differ between countries. Intellectual property rights may be acquired by an organisation which has developed software. If the processing of the software is outsourced to an offshore destination and then refined by the supplier, issues may arise over intellectual property rights, giving rise to potentially complex issues of international law.

Taxation

Care needs to be taken to ensure that the tax implications of an offshore outsourcing contract are fully understood. Local laws may apply and specialist advice should be obtained.

Jurisdiction and applicable laws

By definition, an offshore outsourcing contract involves one or more countries and, therefore, one or more jurisdictions and sets of applicable laws. Jurisdiction is the place where any legal proceedings take place. Applicable law is the law that is applied in the hearing of any dispute.

4: Reaching the Decision

In the European Union (EU) it is possible for an action to arise in the UK, and be adjudicated upon in another EU country. A contract may provide for English law to be applied in the event of a dispute, but this may be overruled by the existence of local laws of the offshore destination.

Employment provisions

Consideration should be given to the provisions of any employment laws in the offshore destination – and where an outsourcing contract provides for more than one offshore destination, the provisions of each should be ascertained. Specialist advice should be obtained.

The culture of the offshore destination may be quite different. Communications may be particularly difficult, to which may be added differences in working and employment procedures and compliance with local employment laws and customs.

Management of relationships during an outsourcing contract, which may last several years, is critical to the success of any outsourcing project and requires an appropriate management infrastructure. Cultural and linguistic differences that tend to arise in offshore outsourcing projects are likely to require the application of particular skills in this respect.

Termination

Careful attention should be paid to the provisions of the contract governing exit strategies. At the end of the contract, the organisation may wish to engage an onshore supplier or another offshore supplier, or bring the function

4: Reaching the Decision

in house. The preservation of intellectual property rights, the obtaining of new, or the transfer of existing, software licences may arise, and local employment laws may apply on termination of the outsourcing contract.

Conclusion

The governance principles of outsourcing projects apply equally to offshore projects as to onshore projects. However, offshore projects present significant additional considerations.

A comprehensive analysis of the complexities of offshore outsourcing considerations is beyond the scope of this book, but it is clear from the issues outlined above that specialist advice from appropriate quarters should be obtained from the outset.

In practical terms, this means that the board should obtain advice before making any decision to outsource to an offshore location. An offshore project is likely to require specialist management resources in place to ensure that the contract is managed satisfactorily for its duration and this may have implications for the business case of outsourcing to an offshore destination.

CHAPTER 5: MODELS OF IT OUTSOURCING

Outsourcing can provide different options for an organisation depending upon the purpose for which it is required. Outsourcing can meet a variety of requirements and can be performed using a variety of methods in order to meet business requirements.

IT outsourcing strategies

Some 'arrangements' that arise between organisation and supplier are considered below under the umbrella of outsourcing. These descriptions can be confusing. Their features are often misunderstood as overlapping variations in their scope emerge:

- The organisation owns the IT assets but a supplier performs the IT function, with the organisation's personnel either on or off the organisation's premises (facilities management).
- The organisation decides on an outsourcing project to maximise its long-term performance (strategic outsourcing).
- Outsourcing is a solution to address a particular issue on a short-term basis (tactical outsourcing).
- The organisation outsources a significant element of its IT function as part of a fundamental re-positioning of the role of IT within the organisation (transitional outsourcing).
- The organisation assigns its in-house IT function to the supplier who is bound by a contract and SLA supported by all the contractual formalities and considerations

5: Models of IT Outsourcing

associated with an external outsourcing project (total outsourcing).

Outsourcing models

There are various methods of performing the outsourcing strategy. Strategies are devised to achieve a specific objective or business goal, the outsourcing model is the framework by which effect is given to the strategy.

The advantages and disadvantages of outsourcing described in the previous chapter apply equally to all outsourcing models. New variants of outsourcing models tend to emerge as new IT solutions develop. It is also clear that the characteristics of each model are sometimes similar and may frequently overlap.

Care must, therefore, be taken to ensure that any model adopted is appropriate to meet the objectives and goals of the organisation.

Application service providers (ASP)

An ASP delivers IT services through a network. Some ASPs supply a single application; others may service specialist clientele, or offer organisation or enterprise-based solutions.

The key features of the model are that the ASP owns and operates the software and supporting servers. The ASP makes the service available via the Internet and bills on a subscription basis, on a 'per user' or monthly fee model. This model emerged several years ago, but after initial interest, failed to generate widespread uptake.

5: Models of IT Outsourcing

Business service provider (BSP)

A BSP offers niche business applications over the Internet. Their applications are provided as web services and delivered securely, employing identity and management protocols and procedures.

Hosted service provider (xSP)

An xSP delivers a wide range of IT functions including applications, but also, for example, security, storage, e-mail services over the Internet. Suppliers may serve many organisations which combine many services with one supplier and have access to a wide range of IT resources.

Managed service provider

This model involves an IT supplier providing specific services on the organisation's premises, so requiring on-site visits, although such services are now frequently provided over the Internet.

The services offered are numerous and can include: network management; remote access; performance management; wireless; virtual private networks; voice solutions; intrusion detection; incident management; business continuity and many more.

Multiple suppliers

This model involves the organisation contracting with a number of suppliers each of which provides an aspect of IT services. They are usually specialist suppliers. Such an

5: Models of IT Outsourcing

arrangement can lead to complex contractual issues arising between the various parties.

Multi-tenancy

This model should not be confused with that of multiple suppliers. Here, the organisation uses software running on the supplier's server. Access to this is offered to numerous other customer organisations known as tenants. It is most frequently a characteristic of Cloud computing (*see section below on Cloud computing*).

Virtual office

This model is based on a single application running on the supplier's server over the Internet as if installed on the organisation's system. It enables the organisation to run 'thin client' or dumb terminal computers thus avoiding the cost of maintaining a large stock of PCs. As an example of this, in the late 1990s, Neil Davidson developed Virtual Solicitors Chambers which provided a centralised IT resource for small law firms requiring the use of legal office IT.

Utility computing

This model involves the supply of IT resources, on a similar concept to metered services provided by public utilities, to meet the use of large numbers of computers on demand.

5: Models of IT Outsourcing

Cloud computing

Of all the IT outsourcing models, Cloud computing is the model that is currently generating most interest. Cloud computing is, perhaps, a third model in the evolution of IT services.

The first, and traditional, stage is the provision of IT services by an in-house IT department. The chief features of this model were considered in Chapter 2. This model is often characterised by limited capacity and complex, expensive IT architecture required for the delivery of a variety of applications required by the organisation. It is 'people' intensive and, therefore, costly to operate.

The second model is the classic, traditional outsourcing model where IT services and, perhaps, IT personnel and assets are outsourced to a supplier. IT services are delivered more effectively by specialist suppliers with greater capacity and at lower cost.

The third model to emerge is Cloud computing. This model provides a service similar to model two, but in a quite different environment.

Definition

Cloud computing involves a variety of outsourcing elements which are constantly changing to meet the demands of parties to IT outsourcing projects. Its key features are the availability of remotely-hosted IT services which may be accessed over the Internet and used in a variety of supply models. Reference to the Cloud arises from the fact that IT services are provided over the Internet without reference to the location of the parties.

5: Models of IT Outsourcing

Most commonly, the model for the supply of such services involves use on demand and payment by subscription on per user or per time bases. It is commonly referred to as a SaaS model. However, confusingly, not all SaaS models are necessarily based on the Cloud model. As various delivery models proliferate the definition becomes more elastic and blurred and the various descriptions can give rise to considerable confusion.

Virtualisation of the supplier's IT resource (*see below*) enables multiple organisations (*see multi-tenants, above*) to have access to the same IT resource.

Dr Richard Sykes[9], independent strategic adviser and elected member of Intellect's main board, says the Cloud model offers ever greater capacity through automated server farms. The 'people' component required for traditional outsourcing services is practically eliminated – as, to a certain extent, is the case where a supplier might well outsource 'on' some of its services to a Cloud supplier.

The greater capacity offered by the Cloud model enables greater volumes of service provision. Economies of scale make the cost of provision significantly cheaper.

Automated processes and the use of virtualisation technology breed a new IT architecture where a supplier provides loosely connected applications, either integrated or stand-alone giving rise to a new service-oriented architecture.

---

[9] Interview: 17 June 2009.

5: Models of IT Outsourcing

Applications from the simple desktop to sophisticated applications are thus highly automated and are provided over the Internet by the supplier.

He argues that because of its speed, simplicity and cost-effectiveness, the Cloud model is both attractive to organisations and a considerable threat to traditional IT service providers. The Cloud model operates without the need for any organisation-based IT infrastructure and, as such, has the potential to offer considerable savings and considerably greater margins of profitability than the traditional outsourcing model.

Payment is not always part of the Cloud model. Facebook and Microsoft® Hotmail® are examples of free Cloud services; and the Cloud model can operate in both internal and external environments.

SaaS and Cloud computing offer a different business model to the traditional model of IT outsourcing. The organisation's focus turns more to the quality of service than the technology itself. In other words, the ability of the supplier to provide modern and sophisticated IT is taken for granted and the organisation becomes far more concerned with the quality, type, convenience, cost-effectiveness and efficiency of service – it is the service that is being sold.

Such has been the proliferation of Cloud computing that in March 2009, the Open Cloud Manifesto was published (*www.opencloudmanifesto.org*). This has the aim of bringing together the Cloud community to recognise and observe a set of core principles and is expressed as being intended for CIOs, governments, IT users, and business leaders and it recognises the immaturity of the Cloud model.

5: Models of IT Outsourcing

The manifesto offers a definition and explains the key features and potential risks. Its principles suggest that Cloud providers should: work together; not lock organisations into their services; and use and adopt existing standards wherever possible.

Virtualisation

Virtualisation is the compartmentalisation of many virtual machines onto a single physical server. This server has the capacity to run numerous applications, systems and infrastructures. As demand for this facility has grown, the cost-effectiveness of the technology has led to the development of server farms and data centres which accommodate vast quantities of data on a hosted basis.

Virtualisation is at the centre of the Cloud model because it enables suppliers to serve multiple organisations without having to assign individual servers for each organisation.

Virtualisation offers benefits in terms of speed, efficiency and cost-savings, and the ability to harness and process limitless quantities of data.

Trends

The trend towards Cloud computing is being propelled by a number of compelling business-related factors. These include the need by organisations to deliver IT applications and solutions in line with market demands. Development cycles of 12 months or even longer are not acceptable commercially, when new versions of applications and solutions become available in a fraction of the time needed

5: Models of IT Outsourcing

by a traditional IT department, enabling internal teams to focus on added value services.

Cloud technology offers agility and dynamic solutions to IT service needs without the need for comprehensive and expensive training programmes. At the same time, the convenience of the Cloud model enables an organisation to monitor, in real-time, the supply of the services as they are required to prevent wasted payment and unmet expectations.

Notable examples of Cloud computing include: Microsoft Azure™; Google Apps™, a package of office applications available over the Internet; the EC2™ service from Amazon®; the rapid rise of the use of business applications provided by Salesforce.com; and IBM's Blue Cloud™.

The rise of interest in Cloud computing is a response to the need of organisations for a dynamic, flexible and agile model for ensuring that IT remains aligned to meeting constantly changing business needs.

One organisation has claimed that its Cloud strategy moved the group from a 95% to 70% operational resource allocation, so freeing up staff and budget to add more value in growth areas; with the aim of freeing up a further 40% of staff and budget to support digital growth.

Another organisation moved low risk, non-business related data to low cost storage tiers presenting the potential to reduce e-mail costs by up to 55%, the equivalent of saving $10 million per annum.

In June 2009, Information Age reported on its website that the success of a server virtualisation project had led Tesco to pursue an almost all-virtual IT infrastructure strategy.

5: Models of IT Outsourcing

Different Cloud computing functions are emerging rapidly. They include infrastructure, platform and application services. At the same time, different models of delivery are being created, so that Cloud users can secure maximum business benefit. These include:

- dedicated services: where a supplier serves one organisation (single tenant);
- volume service: where a supplier serves many organisations (multi-tenant);
- fused services: where a supplier employs a model involving both single and multi-tenants;
- hosted services: where the function is managed and performed in the tenant's organisation.

Benefits

Perhaps the most striking example of the benefits of Cloud computing is illustrated in the potential for efficiency and cost-saving in data management and data storage.

The availability of access to the storage capacity of numerous virtualised data storage facilities obviates the need for the building of data centres and the procurement of machines and software.

The Cloud model offers servers for rent, not ownership, and, therefore, use of the servers, and consequentially, payment can be limited to such times as the organisation requires.

With data storage requirements steadily increasing, the management of all types of data presents a continuing challenge. The Cloud model provides access to storage facilities without the need for up-front payment; and the

5: Models of IT Outsourcing

virtualisation of data servers enables the service to be provided with a comparatively low operational cost.

Other well-recognised benefits include:

- the flexibility of the Cloud model to respond to an organisation's urgent requirements;
- ease and straightforwardness of use;
- the potential to use a variety of Cloud locations; and
- the availability of suppliers who specialise in Cloud services.

There is considerable potential for enormous savings using the Cloud model. For instance, the absence of any need for IT infrastructure, training, systems maintenance, skills updates, licences and upgrades dramatically reduces any IT budget and may even as much as halve it if the contract with the supplier is negotiated effectively.

The Cloud environment is also particularly favourable to start-up organisations wishing to minimise capital expenditure and bolt on new IT applications on an incremental basis and to add capacity over a period of time through ready availability of a wide range of IT solutions.

Transformation

The adoption and subsequent implementation of a Cloud strategy has a number of implications for the management of an organisation's IT strategy. Cloud computing is a disruptive strategy in terms of its effect on the operation of an IT department.

A traditional IT infrastructure involves traditional IT networks operating with the protection of a corporate firewall. The Cloud model involves a network operated by

5: Models of IT Outsourcing

a remotely-based supplier beyond the protection of the traditional corporate firewall. Any organisation moving toward an outsourcing model based on Cloud computing may be required to make fundamental changes to its infrastructure.

This involves a change in management style and structure. Traditional IT staff will not be familiar with the Cloud environment and in any event, their skills may not be required because they are being provided by the supplier. These skills are considered later in the context of the IT department retained by the organisation.

Outsourced IT functions

The diversity of outsourcing strategies and outsourcing models is matched by the rapidly rising number of applications for which outsourcing is regarded as a solution. The variety of outsourcing strategies and the flexibility of the various outsourcing models offer opportunities for organisations of all descriptions to consider outsourcing part or all of their IT function.

In fact, the array of applications that can now be outsourced is arguably too plentiful and can give rise to a degree of confusion between the different types and functions of each solution and their various features.

Computer Economics' *IT Spending, Staffing and Technology Trends 2008/2009*[10] publication lists the

---

[10] *IT Spending, Staffing, and Technology Trends: 2008/2009*, Chapter 6, Computer Economics, Inc. www.computereconomics.com.

5: Models of IT Outsourcing

following applications for which IT outsourcing is now sought:

- Data centre operations
- Help-desk services
- Desktop support
- Application development
- Database administration
- Website and e-commerce
- Data network operations
- Voice network operations
- Disaster recovery services
- IT security.

General research reveals an even wider range of functions which are still likely to be increasing and include:

- Application hosting
- Application management
- Contingency planning
- CRM (customer relationship management)
- Database development
- Database management
- Data warehousing
- Enterprise resource planning
- Hardware support
- Network and systems management
- Networking
- Server operation and management
- Software development
- Staffing
- Storage management
- Wireless.

5: Models of IT Outsourcing

As an example of how intricate the outsourcing process is becoming, services are now offered for the management of the service level agreement for an outsourcing project.

Oblicore[11] is a provider of service level management software which automates, activates and accelerates the monitoring, reporting and management of the service portfolio and service level agreements for enterprises and service providers. The idea is to remove the time-consuming and error prone approach of collection and assembly of service level management data in miscellaneous spreadsheets and custom-built applications.

There presently seems no end to the ingenuity of suppliers in identifying areas of the IT function which organisations are willing and able to contract out. Furthermore, as the IT function is required to respond adequately to the more sophisticated demands of customers, its modular nature will make IT an increasingly popular function to outsource.

Examples of outsourced IT functions

This section examines some examples of various IT functions that can be outsourced, to provide a flavour of the type of function that lends itself to the outsourcing process and to raise awareness of the types of issue that might arise from the perspective of managing the project.

---

[11] www.oblicore.com

5: Models of IT Outsourcing

EDS®

EDS is one of the largest hosting organisations worldwide. Its business process IT outsourcing services include: billing and clearing; card processing; credit; customer relationship management; document processing; HR; insurance; payment and supply management.

McAfee®

McAfee is a global security services provider offering information security solutions to a wide range of organisations. Its total protection solutions offer protection for: desktops and servers, web and e-mail use, data theft, mobile and network and other aspects of data security. It has also developed a series of solutions which are managed on a virtualised model together with Cloud applications, such as remotely operated vulnerability management services; PCI certification compliance; and network security management.

Office Shadow

Office Shadow is based in the USA, UK, and France and provides software (Shadow-Planner) which takes an organisation through the process of business continuity planning. The organisation's data is stored in a central database and is accessible through a web browser. The solution has four aspects: business impact analysis, risk management, business continuity planning and a compliance scorecard.

5: Models of IT Outsourcing

Cloud models

Some of the most prominent suppliers in the Cloud model include: Amazon; Enki; Rackspace and SalesForce.com.

Conclusion

This chapter has examined potential outsourcing strategies, a range of outsourcing models and a variety of IT functions for which outsourcing services are currently available, or being developed, together with some practical examples.

What governance and management issues arise for an organisation considering embarking on an outsourcing strategy?

First, the diversity of IT outsourcing suppliers is considerable. Identifying and selecting a supplier whose solution is precisely aligned with the needs of the business will not be an easy task. Great care will need to be taken over the 'due diligence' process to ensure that the supplier is dependable, financially sound and has the correct management standards in place to provide the level of service required.

Second, the diversity of the location of the supplier raises important compliance implications. The examples above show that locations vary from the USA to India and the UK, while McAfee has offices globally. Any UK organisation wishing to enter into an outsourcing contract with, say, a supplier trading in South America will need to take stringent measures to ensure that any of its data held by the supplier is stored in accordance with the compliance requirements.

5: Models of IT Outsourcing

Third, the range of IT functions for which outsourcing services are now available is comprehensive and seems likely to grow. Some areas are highly specialist. How can an organisation, which will probably be less experienced and less capable of employing the IT to be outsourced, be able to audit satisfactorily a supplier whom it approaches for this service?

Fourth, the organisation must be satisfied that the service to be outsourced is provided to appropriate standards. What evidence should the organisation seek to assure itself that the quality conforms to codes of practice and industry standards?

The common theme arising from these considerations emphasises the need for good governance and sound management. Without a soundly managed strategy in place for implementation of an outsourcing contract, the potential for success is significantly reduced.

CHAPTER 6: PRE-CONTRACT PROCEDURES

This chapter considers the initial stages of the process involved in outsourcing the IT function. These stages call for the development of sound management strategies and accepted management principles.

The need for sound management is essential, not least because of the complexities of outsourcing. The challenges facing the in-house IT department identified in Chapter 2 were: the need to meet competition; the emergence of specialist markets; the need for economies of scale; the overhead cost of an IT department; and compliance issues.

The decision to outsource the IT function introduces a host of business considerations which were considered in Chapter 3 under categories of strategy, technology, compliance, operations and finance. Business considerations must be viewed in the context of the need to align the outsourcing strategy with business goals. It is critical that the process of outsourcing follows a strategy designed to achieve the organisation's business goals.

The complete process is divided into eight processes:

- selection of an outsourcing strategy;
- selection of an outsourcing supplier;
- tendering and negotiations to contract;
- the contract terms and documentation;
- the SLA;
- operational plans for managing the contract;
- post-contract change controls;
- termination of the contract (exit).

6: Pre-contract Procedures

This chapter considers the first three stages. The outsourcing process can involve heavy documentation and become both labour intensive and highly complex. Even in relatively straightforward outsourcing projects, the time taken from the decision to outsource to the implementation of the contract can take several months or even a year or more.

During this period, many teams of different individuals from both organisation and supplier may be involved in the pre-contract process. Throughout this time, the organisation must take care that the project's objectives remain aligned with its original business goals.

Strategy objectives

The board of directors is responsible for setting the organisation's strategies through decision-making processes that follow principles of good governance outlined in the first chapter. The decision to outsource the IT function must be consistent with, and aligned to, its business goals.

The objectives of each organisation in undertaking an IT outsourcing project will be different. They may involve, for example:

- the desire for costs-savings;
- the need for improved service quality to its customers;
- the desire for access to better IT skills and systems;
- an intention to hive-off non-core activities;
- a potential merger or acquisition; or
- a wish to reduce the workforce.

It is for the board to decide the outsourcing model and the type of outsourcing service that will enable the organisation

6: Pre-contract Procedures

to achieve its goals. The contract and the contracting processes are the instruments by which the organisation sets the conditions for achievement of the goals envisaged by the outsourcing of its IT function.

The starting point for the selection of a supplier should be whether its IT skills, services or systems compare sufficiently favourably with any that could be provided by the organisation's in-house IT department. Only if the board decides that there is a sufficiently persuasive case should the project be considered further.

The organisation must also factor in the resources that will be required to manage and administer the relationship with the supplier and to ensure that the contracted services are provided to the required standards. This management function is referred to as the retained IT department – the functions of the IT department that are required during the contract – and is considered later in more detail. Having weighed up the arguments, the board may decide that, with an upgrade of skills or systems, perhaps with the assistance of expert consultancy, it is equally capable of achieving its business goals.

This assessment should be applied to all prospective suppliers to be certain that the engagement of a supplier will complement, and not duplicate the skills and services that the organisation can already offer.

Selection strategy

Having decided to proceed with the project, the board must consider the most suitable type of outsourcing contract. Is a full outsourcing contract required? Does the business strategy warrant one supplier or multiple suppliers? Will

6: Pre-contract Procedures

the project be conducted offshore or at home? Will a single contract suffice or will a series of contracts (a contract framework) be required for multiple suppliers?

In deciding the strategy, it is important not to underestimate the resources that will be required to administer the selection process. An excess of potential suppliers may stretch the resources of management teams and result in inadequate decision-making. Care must be taken that, on the one hand, there are not an undue number of teams or panels assigned to manage the project, and, on the other hand, that adequate resources are deployed.

The criteria for supplier selection will differ according to an organisation's strategy, culture and business goals. Considerations include: the supplier's experience of the organisation's business; the supplier's costs against the value to the organisation; the appearance of a responsive and flexible, positive approach by the supplier; and evidence of conformity to best practices.

Compatibility of cultures is often overlooked. Outsourcing contracts can last for several years and it is, therefore, important that there is a mutual and enduring understanding and respect for each party's approach to the project. Typical cultural issues include:

- **Experience in the market:** the organisation must be satisfied that the supplier has appropriate experience in the marketplace. Typical factors to consider are: history and track record; the nature of its core business; familiarity with the organisation's IT; and client and staffing numbers.
- **Qualifications:** the supplier should be able to demonstrate the necessary skills and competence that will meet the organisation's requirements. Examples

6: Pre-contract Procedures

include: British Standards compliance or the Investors in People standard and general evidence of quality management.

- **Shared vision:** there should be evidence of a shared view of the project and an alignment of expectations, business culture and management strategies. Where the project includes the transfer of personnel, there should be evidence of complementary personnel management and opportunities.
- **Restrictions:** the supplier should be able to demonstrate adaptability in the relevant marketplace and the absence of any relationships that would restrict its abilities to perform the contract and so prevent the organisation realising its objectives.
- **Managing the relationship:** an important element in the success of the project is the ability to manage the relationship. After the contract stage, it will be too late to decide that the relationship is unlikely to work. Some appraisal of the supplier should be made at an early stage.

This will include an assessment of such issues as the supplier's reputation among its customers and the quality of its services and solutions. If personnel are to be included in the outsourcing arrangement, some appraisal and evaluation should be made of the supplier's attitude to the management of personnel.

Whatever criteria the organisation adopts for selecting a supplier, there are two over-riding factors which must be borne in mind throughout the selection process.

First, the prospective supplier must be capable of providing services that support, complement and are compatible with the organisation's business objectives. If this is disregarded, the interests of the parties will diverge and the project will fail, at least from the organisation's perspective.

Second, the organisation must be satisfied that the prospective supplier has adequate knowledge and understanding of its business. A supplier who is unfamiliar with the organisation's area of business is likely to have difficulty meeting the organisation's requirements in a timely, efficient and cost-effective manner. The result will be delay, extra expense and even the need for additional resources while the supplier adjusts to the environment.

Due diligence

Alongside an assessment of the compatibility of the parties' cultures, a formal due diligence process must be undertaken. The due diligence process is of critical importance in identifying and assessing potential risks. In the context of outsourcing the IT function, the significance of properly conducted due diligence processes cannot be overstated.

The outsourcing of the IT function is similar in concept to a sale of part of a business to another party, with the vital difference being that the organisation remains dependent on the supplier's performance for the continuity and profitability of its business.

Such dependency calls for all possible efforts to ensure that due diligence processes are as wide-ranging and comprehensive as possible. The due diligence process in an outsourcing project will normally be conducted during the tendering process when potential suppliers are invited to enter the tendering process.

6: Pre-contract Procedures

The following are some key issues to be addressed in a due diligence exercise. They are not exhaustive because every outsourcing project is different and will be concerned with particular issues.

Strategy

- The corporate identity of the supplier and its ability to contract.
- The geographical location of the supplier.
- Any relationship existing between the supplier and actual or potential competitors.
- Evidence of the supplier's reputation and reliability within the marketplace.
- Evidence of the supplier's ability to respond to new developments in the market.
- Evidence of any need to delegate or outsource part of the function to other suppliers.

Technology

- Evidence of the supplier operating the latest technology.
- Evidence of the supplier having sufficient capacity to accommodate growing requirements of the organisation.
- Evidence of creativity in the development of solutions to meet the needs of end-users.
- Verification of the supplier's IT infrastructure – such as servers, hardware, software and networks.
- Evidence of measures for the assurance of information security and business continuity.

6: Pre-contract Procedures

Compliance

- Evidence of compliance with relevant legislative and regulatory provisions.
- Evidence of observance of relevant industry standards and codes of practice.
- Evidence of adoption of approved standards, such as British Standards or Investors in People.
- Evidence of procedures for managing third-party licences.
- Evidence of procedures for observing compliance processes surrounding data and intellectual property.
- Evidence of any claims against the supplier.

Operations

- Evidence of the processes and procedures of the supplier in servicing the organisation.
- Evidence of any corporate, IT or project governance models observed by the supplier.
- Evidence of technical and other documentary records in respect of all operational activities.
- Evidence of the human resources available to the supplier in the performance of the contract.
- Evidence of employee management procedures.
- Evidence of the skills and qualifications of the supplier's personnel for the supply of the required services.
- Evidence of any industry standards or codes of conduct observed in the management of employees.
- Evidence of internal policies and protocols governing the conduct of employees over, for instance, confidentiality.

6: Pre-contract Procedures

Finance

- Evidence of the financial position and stability of the supplier.
- Evidence from suitably qualified referees as to the financial suitability of the supplier for the provision of the proposed services.
- Evidence of financial and/or performance guarantees.
- Evidence of any bank or company guarantees.
- Evidence of any relevant policies of insurance and other documentation.

Financial due diligence should be distinguished from a financial audit. An audit examines historical data only. Due diligence concerns historical, current and future trends against the business plan of the supplier and the viability of the proposed application. The types of issue that a financial due diligence process encompasses include: historical current and future data; availability of capital; loans and guarantees; liabilities to employees; tax liabilities; the validity of asset valuations and risks that are revealed in the process.

An area that is now receiving increasing attention is the problem of checking the quality of the supplier's security controls in respect of data received from the organisation. The organisation has the right to perform, or engage an expert organisation to perform, an audit of the supplier's security systems and processes; audit checks should be raised at the due diligence stage and included in the tendering documentation and later as a provision of the contract.

Adequate strategic, technological, compliance, operational and financial checks are fundamental to an effective due

6: Pre-contract Procedures

diligence exercise. As each outsourcing contract is different, the organisation should not overlook other areas particular to the proposed project. The effort and resources required for an effective due diligence exercise should not be underestimated.

Cloud computing

These due diligence checks also apply to Cloud computing projects. However, in Cloud computing projects, data handling issues require particular consideration. Although an organisation's data may pass to the supplier, under the DPA, the organisation, as data controller, is still responsible for compliance with the obligations the legislation imposes. These obligations are considered in detail later.

First, where data is being transferred to the supplier's data centre, evidence of a certified physical and technological audit should be sought.

Second, evidence should be obtained of the skills, competence and trustworthiness of the supplier's employees, together with employment policies and any standards with which the supplier is accredited.

Third, evidence should be obtained concerning all who may have access to the data, particularly in the case of a multi-tenanted Cloud model.

Fourth, evidence should be obtained over the general management of the organisation's data, for instance:

- back-up, consents to transfer to third parties;
- legal compliance issues;
- electronic discovery procedures;
- preservation of data;

6: Pre-contract Procedures

- jurisdictions in which the data may be held or to which it may be transferred;
- compliance with local laws and regulations; and
- compliance with data protection provisions in respect of any transfer.

Some commentators believe that the development of the Cloud computing model will be significantly inhibited by the reluctance of organisations to enter into Cloud contracts because of the inability or refusal of Cloud suppliers to provide adequate information on compliance, security and general risk issues.

Tendering and negotiations

Because of the resource implications of managing this process, it is sensible to confine the shortlist to two or three potential suppliers.

SHL (_www.shl.com_) is a global human resources supplier and has outsourced virtually the whole of its IT function. Andy McCallum[12], Service Delivery Director, believes developing a relationship with prospective suppliers during the tendering process is critical.

We spent lots of time with the short-listed bidders both formally and socially so we could find out as much as possible about them and whether they would fit in with our culture. We spent six months or so on this process because we felt the issue of compatibility was so important.

It seemed to us that you get out of a relationship what you put into it.

---

[12] Interview: 18 June 2009.

6: Pre-contract Procedures

Short-listing involves the process of a request for information (RFI) required by the organisation from potential suppliers with the aim of providing the required standard of service for the required value in a mutually beneficial arrangement. The organisation will need to provide an outline of the services it requires. The information required will identify such issues as:

- the type of work undertaken for customers;
- the technology employed;
- disaster recovery services;
- support and training for personnel involved;
- financial issues, such as accounts, turnover and profitability; and
- details of any other outsourcing contracts.

From this information, it should be possible to move towards the selection of potential suppliers. This involves sending a request for proposals (RFP) or an invitation to tender (ITT) to each potential supplier with a view to entering the tendering process.

The tender documentation is intended to describe the organisation, its core activities and its business strategy. It is sensible to explain why and how the decision to outsource has been taken. It is important that potential suppliers are provided with as much information as possible so the organisation gains a true impression from its responses.

Tender documentation typically includes: details of the organisation; service requirements; personnel issues; assets included in the project; charging proposals; security requirements and proposals for the contract. It is good practice to attach a draft of the contract and SLA to the

6: Pre-contract Procedures

tender documents, so that potential bidders can make a decision at an early stage on whether they can meet the organisation's requirements.

The tender documentation will contain data that is sensitive for the organisation. A potential bidder should be required to sign a non-disclosure agreement (NDA) to address both the fact of the negotiations and any information disclosed. Signing an NDA signifies a commitment by the bidder that they, and any third party that may be involved, will preserve the confidentiality of the data.

The ITT will contain key points of the project. If an interim agreement is entered into as part of the tendering process, legally it is a valid contract and may give rise to the need for further negotiations.

During the tendering process, a sensible negotiating strategy is for the organisation to maintain competition for as long as possible to achieve a contract on the best terms possible. Where negotiations take place with multiple bidders, an assessment may be needed over whether the cost and effort of the process is practical on the basis of the resources required.

In any outsourcing negotiations, there are three components to address: rights and liabilities issues, IT infrastructure issues, and commercial issues.

- **Rights and obligations:** typical factors to address include: intellectual property rights; licences; warranties and indemnities; personnel; the parties' liabilities; and contract exit.
- **IT infrastructure:** these factors concern the scope of the contract and include: contract conditions; remedies (such as service credits); data and change management.

- **Commercial issues:** these factors define the scope of the services, critical events that release the parties from their obligations under the contract and any sums payable on termination.

Only when the respective bidders' positions on all issues arising within these components are clearly established should consideration be given to any submitted bids.

While negotiations progress, the organisation should be conducting a due diligence process in order to establish whether there are any restrictions that affect its ability to outsource – such as contracts with other parties, software licences, and any impediment on the transfer of assets, or personnel.

In respect of its personnel, the organisation will need to consider employees' rights under the provisions of the Assigned Rights Directives and TUPE 2006. These are discussed in detail later.

Account should be taken of the length of time that the tendering and negotiation processes may take. These processes invariably take longer than either party anticipates at the outset. Therefore, in calculating the pre-operative period, allowance should be made for 'slippage'. It is not unusual for the total process, depending on the complexity of the project, to take a year or more.

It is equally important for the organisation to prepare the documentary stages of the process at the earliest possible stage. Delayed submission of documents by bidders will inevitably lengthen the process.

Negotiating tactics define the organisation-supplier relationship and will help the organisation learn how the supplier behaves in the business environment. It should also

6: Pre-contract Procedures

be remembered that negotiations are not confined to the pre-contract stage of the process, but will arise in the event, for instance, of changes, disputes and during the exit procedure.

Negotiation approaches are either based on maximising the value of shared interests or they are positional – seeking a better bargain. Successful negotiation will involve a combination of the two. An over-competitive approach may affect the future balance of the relationship and, therefore, jeopardise the long-term effectiveness of the project.

CHAPTER 7: THE CONTRACT

The contract represents the agreement between the parties and governs their legal and business relationship. It is a legally binding document and provides the framework for the management and operation of the outsourcing project. The contract defines the services to be provided and the respective responsibilities of the parties.

Reasons for a contract

The contract has a number of important functions:

- it is the backdrop against which negotiations are conducted;
- it is a potential risk management tool which provides for methods of avoiding and resolving disputes;
- it provides the organisation with rights and remedies when required against a supplier; and
- it is an overriding framework which governs the conduct of the parties.

Care must, therefore, be taken to ensure that the parties to the contract are correctly identified (for example, a subsidiary company as opposed to a holding company) and are also legal entities entitled to enter into legally binding contracts. A contract by a company is executed with a company seal. If a third party is involved, a separate contract with the third party is required.

It is important to provide as much information as possible at the earliest stage, so that the supplier is not ambushed by contract and service requirements at a late stage which

7: The Contract

causes delay. It is good practice for a draft of the proposed contract to accompany the ITT documentation.

Contract construction

The main contract

The contract comprises different components of which the principal component is the main body of the contract. This document contains formal provisions governing the arrangements between the parties, such as:

- details of the parties;
- the general services to be supplied;
- the supplier's costs and other charges;
- any assets to be transferred;
- any personnel to be transferred;.
- the duration of the contract;
- change management needs that might arise during the contract term;
- data protection and general confidentiality provisions;
- jurisdictional and applicable law provisions;
- liability (or exclusion) for representations;
- complaint management mechanisms;
- provisions for audit of the supplier's performance;
- consequences of the supplier's substandard performance;
- provisions limiting the parties' liabilities and indemnities;
- provision for the supplier's insolvency; and
- provision for the resolution of disputes.

There may be additional provisions to govern the special needs of the parties according to nature of the IT function to be outsourced. If the detail of all these provisions were to

7: The Contract

be included in one document, the contract would become unmanageably complex. In order to avoid this, the main contract is supplemented by schedules which govern particular aspects of the parties' arrangements more specifically.

Three important areas of the contract require special mention: service management, personnel transfer and asset transfer.

Service management

The main contract will outline the services to be provided, but specific details will be set out in the schedules. Included in the main contract will be reference to such issues as: optional or extra services; transition plans; relevant quality standards; timescales and business continuity; and disaster recovery provisions.

Also included will be provision for the management of the services to be provided, such as the parties' management teams, performance standards and audits.

The main contract will also govern the issue of the supplier's charges. Issues the contract will address include: payment procedures and changes in charges. The detail of the supplier's actual charges will be contained in a schedule.

Transfer of personnel

The outsourcing project may involve the outsourcing of some, or all, personnel in the IT department. If so, the contract should contain reference to the personnel involved. The details will be set out in the schedule and should

7: The Contract

include the number of staff to be transferred, length of employment, details of salaries, accrued benefits and existing terms and conditions.

The legal position regarding personnel transferred under an outsourcing contract is governed by the TUPE 2006 regulations (*see Chapter 18, page 286*).

Transfer of assets

Any assets to be transferred to the supplier as part of the contract will be specified. Examples of such assets include: hardware and software; network equipment; licences; support agreements; contractor contracts; employment policies; insurance policies and leases – but will depend on each project. Broadly, any item or documentation relevant to the performance of the contract should be regarded as an asset, identified in the contract and detailed in the schedule.

Intellectual property rights (IPR) are assets which represent some original creation by one or more individuals or corporate bodies. IPR in software are often overlooked and can cause particular problems. If software is to be transferred by an organisation holding IPR, a licence should be issued in respect of each piece of software concerned.

It can sometimes be difficult to identify the ownership of software correctly because of its diverse origins from:

- the organisation's personnel;
- in-house personnel and contactors jointly;
- commissions from external developers;
- a third-party distributor or contactor; or
- creation for a mass market.

7: The Contract

The correct licences must be obtained and issued to the supplier for the purposes of any transfer.

Only the owner or creator of the software can enforce IPR against unauthorised users through the Copyright Designs and Patents Act 1988 (CDPA). For a fee, software houses issue licences to users. Although software licences are the most common mechanism, it is also possible to assign ownership of copyright to another party by agreement.

Licences may impose conditions on the way the software is to be used, for example, limiting numbers, or setting fees by reference to the number of users.

If the organisation owns the copyright in software to be outsourced, a licence should be granted to the supplier limited to use for the purposes of the outsourcing contract.

If the supplier owns the software to be used in the outsourcing project, a problem may arise for the organisation at the end of the outsourcing contract. The organisation should, therefore, obtain a licence for use of the software after the end of the contract, if necessary, for use by another supplier.

If a third party owns the software, a check should be made to ensure that the outsourcing of any software used by the organisation which is to be transferred does not infringe any restriction in the original software licence granted to the organisation. Usually, licences will allow for use only by the organisation and will specify that the third party retains ownership. This is to avoid situations where the organisation might issue a licence to a supplier who turns out to be a competitor of the third party.

The use of software without a licence from the owner exposes the user to potential criminal proceedings and a

7: The Contract

claim for damages for breach of copyright, although the making of back-up copies for lawful use is permitted under the section 50 A (1) of the Copyright (Computer Program) Regulations 1992.

Steps should be taken to obtain any necessary licences and permissions at the earliest possible stage. The first step is to identify what software is to be used and who holds the IPR. The first issue is relatively straightforward, but the second may require some investigation, especially in the case of legacy software, or software of which the origins are unclear.

Once these enquiries are satisfied, the authorisation process should begin immediately to allow for any difficulties in obtaining licences. It is not advisable to enter into a contract for the use of software until the position regarding any licences has been clearly established. If, after entering into a binding contract, a user is found to be using software without a licence, proceedings for damages and an injunction may be issued by the software owner which, in turn, might prejudice the performance of the contract and raise legal issues between the organisation and the supplier.

For this reason, the contract should include an indemnity clause by which the organisation contracts with the supplier to indemnify the supplier in respect of any third party claims for loss or expenses for any infringements of the third party's IPR.

Where an original software solution is developed during the outsourcing solution by the supplier, any modification or development of the organisation's original software normally means the organisation will retain the IPR. Where the issue is not capable of resolution between the parties, an escrow agreement may provide for the source

7: The Contract

code to be deposited with a third party, most usually to cover the eventuality of the insolvency of the supplier (*see Chapter 18, page 285*).

Contract schedules

The main body of the contract contains the substantive agreement between the parties. However, the nature of an outsourcing project has many different features and as each outsourcing project is different, each contract will have a wide and varied range of provisions in order to reflect the parties' intentions.

The mechanism for addressing this complexity is the schedule. Effectively, each schedule is in the nature of a sub-contract which may specify particular applications or services to be supplied or may amplify or qualify certain terms of the contract. Examples of typical categories for consideration in schedules include:

- **Security:** this category addresses issues relating to the security protocols, procedures and mechanisms – both physical and electronic – to be adopted by both parties.
- **Management:** this category addresses management issues, transition procedures; change management; contract management; complaint, dispute resolution and escalation processes; exit procedures; disaster recovery and business continuity procedures.
- **Performance and audits:** this category addresses issues, such as service requirements; service levels; performance reports; and standard and quality of service.
- **Finance:** this category addresses charging issues, the supplier's charges and expenses; payment methods and mechanisms; and payment arrangements.

- **Administration:** this category addresses issues, such as identification of assets included in the contract; the identification of any licences to be obtained; identification and summary of terms of employment of any personnel to be transferred under the contract; and escrow agreements.

Multiple-outsourcing

The need for more specialist IT solutions has led to the increasing development of outsourcing to more than one supplier. The more sophisticated demands of customers often means that more than one IT solution is needed, which may be beyond the capability of one supplier. Specialist functions are also evident, such as back-office, payroll management and accounting services.

Other factors that fuel the demand for multi-sourcing include outsourcing of central parts of the business process to different (global) locations, or a wish by the organisation to avoid becoming too dependent on one supplier.

Multiple-sourcing involves obtaining IT services from a number of service providers who integrate their services within a contractual and governance framework. The full contracting procedure must be adopted in respect of each supplier because a legal relationship arises in each case.

Multiple-sourcing gives rise to a number of considerations.

Culture

Care should be taken to ensure as far as possible that there is a similar business and ethical culture between the organisation and all suppliers, particularly to avoid an over-

7: The Contract

competitive approach by some suppliers. It is important that each supplier understands and shares the organisation's and other suppliers' objectives for the project.

Services

The contract should define precisely the range of services to be provided by each supplier, so as to avoid disputes at a later stage in the project. Where the range of services is diverse, it may be more practical for a general contract to be issued, but with schedules that tailor the contract to the needs of specific suppliers.

Accountability

The contract should specify and define the respective legal responsibilities, accountabilities and liabilities of each party under the contract. Specifically, this should include:

- the suppliers' respective obligations to the organisation and each other over the handling of data belonging to the organisation and other suppliers;
- NDAs and confidentiality clauses observed by all parties to the contract to ensure the confidentiality of information shared during the project; and appropriate indemnity clauses to protect the organisation;
- stipulations in the contract that the suppliers will integrate their services to provide a seamless service, and co-operate with each other during the project;
- appropriate indemnity clauses from the suppliers to protect the organisation in respect of any one or more suppliers failing to provide the contracted services to the agreed standard;

- procedures for determining disputes between the suppliers over the provision of the contracted services.

Management

Managing multiple supplier contracts has significant additional features and is an important management resource factor in considering whether to outsource using this model.

If a major reason for multiple outsourcing is to save cost, there may be a corresponding increase in expenditure in retaining or recruiting competent personnel in the organisation to provide an appropriate management team, for example, the appointment of one or more project managers.

Common strategies for managing the relationship between the parties in order to maintain co-operation and ensure fair treatment include:

- appointing a lead supplier;
- ensuring suppliers are reliant on each other;
- establishing similar standards for each supplier; and
- ensuring each supplier appreciates:
  - the component services of the project;
  - how these components integrate;
  - the respective relationships within the project; and
  - their respective roles and responsibilities.

Implementing good governance principles is of particular importance for the successful management of a multiple supplier contract. Here, the need for a clear strategy, lines of accountability and responsibility is essential; and robust

7: The Contract

compliance, risk management and implementation standards are paramount.

A management framework that ensures these principles are applied is equally necessary. In such a case, the organisation and each supplier should establish standard complementary management structures which operate to consistent standards at all levels of the project in respect of:

- meetings;
- lines of operational and management accountability;
- monitoring;
- reporting procedures;
- auditing; and
- dispute escalation.

Key success factors

What are the key issues for satisfactory implementation of the contracting process?

As in any project, preparation is vital for success. Even though an organisation may be experienced in managing outsourcing projects, no two outsourcing projects are the same. Each will have different considerations.

Preparation

Early and thorough preparation is essential. All data necessary for the preparation of the contract and schedules should be available at the earliest opportunity. The potential length of the pre-contract period may be significant and the longer the delay, the greater the likelihood that pre-contract negotiations become stale and subsequently fail, or result in an unsatisfactory contract.

In the period of negotiation before the contract, an organisation may overlook the fact that eventually the project will come to an end. Even though the termination date may be far off, it is sensible for the organisation to consider as far as possible how it might be placed. Will it wish to rely on a retained IT department and continue outsourcing arrangements with the proposed supplier or other suppliers? Will the organisation consider taking the IT function in house?

Although definite decisions will not be possible at this stage, the organisation should ensure that the contract is as flexible as possible to allow for as many contingencies as possible at the exit stage.

Culture

The tendering, negotiation and contract stages are likely to indicate the culture and relationship between parties during the project. During these stages, it is important to pay close attention to the development of the relationship and to cultivate collaborative and team working arrangements wherever possible. Prompt attention to potential problems will help to assess the correct steps needed for future management of areas of disagreement.

Business goals

Throughout the pre-contract period, especially during the due diligence process and the need to understand the implications of complex contractual documentation, the organisation may temporarily overlook the original purpose of the project. Throughout this potentially long and protracted process, care must be taken not to lose sight of the strategy goals that the outsourcing project is intended to address.

Cloud computing contracts

Contracting in the Cloud computing environment is far less formal than the traditional outsourcing project. Speaking at a recent webinar, a representative of a major Cloud computing supplier made the comment that Cloud computing contracting was far simpler than contracting in the traditional model and there was no need for lawyers or complex documentation!

In the traditional model, the organisation is advised to include a draft of the outsourcing contract with the tendering documentation in order that the supplier is fully appraised of the services and standards required by the organisation.

In the traditional environment, the initiative in the contracting process rests with the organisation in arriving at the eventual agreement between the parties. While the organisation cannot dictate the terms agreed between the parties, the framework of its contract can nevertheless indicate that the organisation is driving the initiative.

Cloud computing contracts are prepared and provided by the supplier and issued to the organisation intending to use its services. The dynamic shifts from the traditional model, in which the organisation drives the process, to the Cloud model where the process is controlled by the supplier.

7: The Contract

At present, there does not seem to be a standard form of contract recognised and approved by any professional or standards-based organisation for the framework and content of Cloud computing contracts.

A consequence of this is that any contract prepared by the supplier may reasonably be expected to be more favourable to the supplier in its construction and content, than to the prospective organisation. In such circumstances, contrary to the suggestion of the speaker in the webinar, any organisation embarking on a Cloud computing project is strongly urged to seek legal advice on any contract or terms of business submitted by a supplier.

Even if the supplier refuses to amend those terms of the contract which are considered unfavourable, at least the legal adviser will explain the full implications of the contract, so that the organisation enters any agreement fully aware of its legal position.

As there is no standard form of Cloud computing contract, what form might it take and what might be its key provisions? Typically, the contract might address the issues below.

A summary overview

This confirms the parties to the contract and outlines: the nature and scope of the services; the basis of the terms of engagement; the obligation of the organisation to make payment in terms agreed between the parties; and a general reference to termination.

7: The Contract

Intellectual property

This provision will set out the parties' respective rights and responsibilities with regard to any rights in any intellectual property created during the project. It contains provisions governing the rights of use and/or distribution of any intellectual property and the requirement for confidentiality.

The organisation's position

This addresses the organisation's position over, for instance:

- the organisation's co-operation;
- best practice in the handling of data;
- payment periods and methods of payment;
- confidentiality over the agreement between the parties;
- the provision of an indemnity for any misuse of the supplier's system by the organisation; and
- the procedure for termination by the organisation.

The supplier's position

This addresses the supplier's position over, for instance:

- commitment to providing satisfactory service;
- commitment to fair and proper complaints-handling;
- use of customer information;
- use of the organisation's intellectual property created in the course of the project;
- provisions regarding shared data;
- confidentiality of the organisation's data;
- warranty as to standards of service;
- limitations of liability;

7: The Contract

- termination provisions; and
- provisions for arbitration and jurisdiction in disputes.

A Cloud computing contract may also include provisions governing the use of the service by the organisation, either in the main contract or as a schedule. This may stipulate that the organisation will use the service for business purposes only and not abuse the service in any way. From the supplier's perspective, this is understandable. In a multi-tenant environment in particular, the supplier is faced with possibly numerous organisations loading data of all descriptions and from all sources onto its server farm. The potential for infected or illegal data is significant, and is addressed by a series of provisions governing the export of data from an organisation onto its systems.

From the organisation's perspective, these provisions are a timely reminder to its personnel of the need for compliance with organisational policies on the purity, security and legality of data and data-handling.

Such provisions may forbid, for instance, the loading of data that:

- is illegal;
- is pornographic;
- is contaminated with malware or spyware;
- infringes any intellectual property rights;
- abuses or compromises the supplier's system;
- is used for unsolicited marketing purposes; or
- is stored without licence.

Every Cloud computing contract is different and will have different requirements and provisions to meet the parties' requirements.

7: The Contract

The approach of a Cloud computing contract differs significantly from that of a traditional outsourcing contract. This flows from the fact that the dominant commercial position seems to move from organisation to supplier.

The terms of the supplier's contract will be much less sympathetic to the organisation than a traditional contract prepared by the organisation. There will be much less inclination for the supplier serving a multi-tenant mass-market to accommodate the individual preferences of the organisation, simply because in any mass market the supplier is generally dominant until a predominant section of the market is sufficiently collectively assertive to challenge this. If this has not already developed, in due course, one can foresee the emergence of an international Cloud computing users association to assert the rights of its members against suppliers.

For the time being, however, organisations should beware of the lure of significantly lower computing charges and remember the governance principles set out in Chapter 1 – transparency, responsibility, accountability, shareholder and stakeholder value, and, critically, risk management.

CHAPTER 8: THE SERVICE LEVEL AGREEMENT

The SLA defines the agreement between the parties over the scope of the project, the levels of service to be provided and the supplier's charges for performance of the contract. The SLA is a schedule to the main contract. The three key areas are service levels, scoping and pricing.

As a matter of general law, the supplier has a duty to use reasonable skill and care in the performance of the agreement, but the SLA defines the supplier's obligations much more precisely.

Service levels

The objective of the SLA is to define the obligations of the parties regarding the performance of the main contract. It governs the operational relationship between the parties.

The SLA is a document that specifies agreed service levels which are subject to a continuous process of monitoring, reporting and reviews. The supplier will have knowledge of the capability of its IT solutions and should, therefore, take the lead in defining the service levels in the first instance.

In order to create service levels, there must be a clear understanding of the services required. Current service levels should be established from relevant data and a 'gap' analysis should be performed, so that the new SLA complements the existing service level. At the same time, potential improvements in service levels arising from automation can be identified and the final service level proposed can be included in the tendering process.

8: The Service Level Agreement

Andrew Giverin[13] suggests three service level examples:

- Continuous measurement: service levels which are measured on a continuous basis;
- Event-based: measures for all events completed in the measurement period; whether the event was completed correctly on time;
- Sampling: service level which measures a sample to confirm whether the sample meets a required standard.

The agreed service levels should be promulgated to relevant personnel within the organisation, so that expectations are understood and any discrepancies can be acted upon immediately.

Service levels should be all-inclusive. The SLA is a contract for which any breach will be enforceable by penalties and, as a last resort, actionable at law. It cements expectations, obligations and responsibilities. It operates as a guarantee of meeting the demands of the organisation and its customers.

Service levels should be measurable and realistic, and should relate to substantive requirements. Vague and generalist aspirations that can lead to confusion and disputes should be avoided. Allowances should be made for holidays and illnesses.

As quality of service is at the heart of service levels, a prudent organisation might insist on compliance with a relevant industry standard, for example, ISO9001.

---

[13] *From cradle to grave – the outsourcing lifecycle: seminar*, Giverin A, Society for Computers & Law, 12 February 2009.

8: The Service Level Agreement

The supplier will be responsible for maintaining performance statistics and reporting to the organisation with supporting data at agreed intervals.

The organisation may decide to prioritise some services in which case a schedule of the degree of priority of service provision should be provided to the supplier.

Scope

The scope of the SLA is the quality of the service – that is what is provided, not the process by which it is to be delivered. The organisation and its customers are interested in results, not procedures. It is important that the scope is clarified precisely at the outset to avoid ambiguities and misunderstanding at later stages of the project.

Care should be taken to specify precisely the responsibilities for each function and ensure that responsibilities for intermediate functions within a specific process are not overlooked.

The SLA is the principal management tool by which the organisation manages the performance of the contract and should give priority to the needs of the organisation. It should define all levels of service to be provided in order to ensure a consistent standard of provision in respect of all contracted services.

In an IT outsourcing contract, defining scope does not necessarily involve explaining the technology in question, but it will involve explaining the function it performs as it is the standard of performance upon which the organisation relies.

8: The Service Level Agreement

Pricing

In order to be effective, a pricing strategy must have certain requirements. The price of the service must be certain and based on a realistic understanding of the practicalities of the performance required. A price that does not provide value or is not related to performance will ultimately defeat the object of the SLA.

The pricing model must reflect the services provided in objectively measured quantities, applying correct pricing levels and reflecting the service levels to be achieved. Care should be taken that the pricing structure does not inadvertently reward poor service. There should be regular pricing reviews to allow for changes in the market, future automation and efficiencies in production.

SLA framework

Depending on the service to be provided, there may be one or more SLAs. The SLA must be easily understood by those using it, so an assessment should be made of the main user groups who will be involved.

This may include, for instance, boards of directors and senior managers, end-users or specific user groups. The wide range of potentially interested parties means that the SLA should be expressed in easily understood terms.

Each SLA will be different because outsourcing projects differ from one another but there are common areas to be addressed in any SLA. Where special provisions are required, they will fall to be negotiated.

8: The Service Level Agreement

Introduction

This provides the names of the parties, a brief description of the service and the duration of the SLA.

Service

This will cover:

- the service and the parties' respective responsibilities;
- the anticipated levels of use;
- the support facilities available during the contract; and
- agreed periods when the service will not be provided.

Security

This will cover:

- the measures securing electronic data;
- business continuity plans;
- conformity with relevant legislation; and
- compliance with current industry standards force.

Performance

This area addresses agreed performance levels and covers:

- levels and volumes of use of the service;
- service provision levels;
- key performance indicators;
- management and monitoring reports;
- performance reviews;
- performance integration with other suppliers; and
- incident reporting and resolution procedures;

8: The Service Level Agreement

- agreed targets for problem/incident resolution.

Costs and charges

This will cover:

- payment processes and procedures;
- agreed terms for payments;
- the charges to be made; and
- financial penalties and service credits.

Dispute resolution

This will cover:

- escalation processes and procedures;
- referrals for arbitration or mediation.

Other provisions may address consultation with user groups during the SLA and the incorporation of periodic amendments to the SLA.

Service credits are sums agreed in the SLA that will be paid to the organisation in the event of the supplier defaulting on one or more service levels. They operate as an incentive for the supplier and compensation for the organisation. They are one remedy, among others, which include escalation, dispute resolution and, as a last resort, legal action for breach of contract.

Escalation is a process whereby a dispute is referred to senior levels of management for resolution in the event of resolution failing at lower management levels. It is sensible for each party to have comparable escalation management

8: The Service Level Agreement

levels, so that, if the procedure is invoked, similar levels of management experience and qualification address the issue.

The SLA is a critical tool in the contracting procedure. It governs the performance and operation of the contract. If properly implemented, it is a valuable tool for the effective management of the organisation's relationship with the supplier. An SLA which is negotiated in such a way that it subsequently proves unworkable or unmanageable by either party is a quick route to an early breakdown of the relationship between the parties.

Cloud computing SLAs

A Cloud computing contract may also be supported by an SLA. This is frequently included within the contract. Typically, this will specify the supplier's commitment to providing facilities, but may be less detailed on the level of service to be provided under the contract.

Three areas that these types of SLA may address include:

- the specification of its servers, guaranteed minimum periods in respect of any downtime and the consequential financial arrangements in this event;
- the specification of its network, guaranteed minimum periods in respect of any downtime and the consequential arrangements in this event; and
- scheduled downtime on notification to the organisation without provision of compensation.

SLA specifications in a Cloud computing contract may be much less specific than those in a traditional contract. It should be remembered that the SLA will have been provided by the supplier and may, therefore, contain

8: The Service Level Agreement

provisions more favourable to the supplier. The organisation should beware of limitation clauses which severely curtail the organisation's right to compensation in the event of outages or inadequate service provision.

CHAPTER 9: MANAGING THE CONTRACT, THE SLA AND THE TRANSITION

Effective management of the contract is critical to the success of an IT outsourcing project. Contract management goes beyond ensuring compliance with the terms of the contract and the contract schedules. It also includes management of the relationship between the organisation and the supplier. An outsourcing arrangement may continue for several years and it is, therefore, important to create an enduring relationship.

There are three areas to be considered in respect of the management of the contract:

- management of the contract;
- management of the SLA; and
- management of the relationship between organisation and supplier.

Managing the contract

If the contract is to be managed effectively, there must be a clear understanding of the respective roles and responsibilities of both organisation and the supplier.

It is important to remember the parties' different objectives. The organisation wants to improve profitability, its services to customers, and competitiveness; the supplier wants to develop more business by generating goodwill and wants to make adequate profit. At the same time, the organisation needs to retain a degree of control to ensure that the contact enables it to meet its business objectives.

9: Managing the Contract, the SLA and the Transition

The foundation for sound contract management is based on a clear mutual understanding of the parties' roles and responsibilities under the contract. This will be achieved through appropriate management appointments, agreed protocols for contract discussions and sound communication strategies.

The functions of managing the contract should not be confused with those required for management of the SLA. The former are more strategic in nature and will be concerned with the overall project; the latter will focus on the operation of the service itself.

Typical management functions relating to the contract might include: contract changes and amendments; resolution of financial issues; handling dispute resolution; and reviews of objectives. The organisation must ensure that, during its lifetime, the contract remains aligned with its business objectives.

The wide spectrum of contract management functions requires suitably skilled personnel, especially in the case of the contract manager. The following are the main skills required for this position:

- an understanding of financial management both within and beyond the organisation;
- an awareness of technology, particularly an understanding of the potential for IT innovation;
- an ability to conduct negotiations at a senior level;
- a broad understanding of the legal issues concerning the contracting of outsourcing IT services;
- a capability for problem-solving and an understanding of the principles of mediation; and

9: Managing the Contract, the SLA and the Transition

- an ability to lead and manage people both in teams and individually.

Such a formidable array of competence calls for an individual unlikely to hold a position below that of senior manager. This is a critical position because it is the sound management of the contract upon which the success or failure of the project largely depends.

Managing the SLA

The management of the SLA is concerned with operational issues, that is, the actual performance of the supplier under the agreement.

This function should not overlap or conflict with the contract management function, because, in that event, confusion would inevitably arise over the parties' roles and responsibilities in managing the whole project and key issues would doubtless be overlooked.

Non-compliance with the SLA can be very damaging to the success of the outsourcing contract. The SLA goes to the very essence of the parties' expectations. Non-compliance can result in reduced productivity, higher labour costs, additional expense and an unsatisfactory service to the end-user. Negative publicity arising from substandard performance may result in reputational damage to either, or both, parties. A properly managed SLA effectively binds the parties to agreed standards and management processes. It is important to understand the critical components of success and apply measurable objectives for their achievement.

9: Managing the Contract, the SLA and the Transition

Management of the SLA should not be applied heavy-handedly. Objectives should be relevant to the parties' desired outcomes and the focus should be on all, but only, the required data.

There must be room for variation in an SLA. Requirements may change at frequent intervals. IT is well known for its ever-changing pace of development.

The SLA should be a model reflecting the right kind of behaviour – or governance – between the parties in giving effect to the contract.

It is important to understand the two distinct aspects of managing the SLA: managing the *provision* of the service, and managing the *level* of the service, to be provided by the supplier – and that these aspects apply to each SLA that forms a schedule to the main contract.

Service provision

This function has a more strategic feel to it than managing the service level, even if it is strictly speaking an operational function. Service provision may change from time to time as the needs of the organisation changes. For this reason, management of the provision of the service involves a more collaborative approach.

Typical functions will include:

- planning meetings with the supplier to consider the existing and potentially new services;
- reviews and monitoring of all SLAs;
- addressing internal and external issues that may impact on the type of services being provided; and

9: Managing the Contract, the SLA and the Transition

- the relevance of quality standards to the service provision.

Each organisation will have different requirements and issues affecting service provision will, therefore, be particular to each contract. The main point to bear in mind is that this is essentially an overview of the services to be provided.

Service levels and metrics

This function addresses the effectiveness of the service being provided. The process focuses on describing and defining the levels (or standards) of service expected by the organisation that will address the needs of its end-users. The objective is to obtain clear and consistent levels throughout the lifetime of the contract.

Typical issues to which particular attention should be paid include: targets, measurable objectives, improvements and innovations, supported by appropriate monitoring and review processes. These issues are measured by a series of metrics agreed between organisation and supplier and included as part of the SLA.

From the perspective of the organisation, the purpose of metrics is to ensure supplier compliance with the contract; in turn, ensuring that the outsourcing project meets the organisation's strategic objectives. Metrics should be set, so that they fall within the competence of the supplier, in other words, they must be realistic or performance disputes will soon arise. Metrics should be relevant, capable of analysis, and consistently applied; yet, at the same time, care should be taken to ensure that metrics are not too complex.

9: Managing the Contract, the SLA and the Transition

From this, it follows that care should be taken at the tendering and due diligence stage to set out the basic metrics required by the organisation, so that checks can be made that the supplier can perform to the required levels.

What are the types of area with which the board will be particularly concerned in assessing metrics?

- **Strategically:** the board will wish to ensure that metrics are set, so that the contract is performed to enable the organisation to achieve its business goals.
- **Technologically:** the board will wish to consider volumes, responsiveness, efficiency, and quality with end-users' experience uppermost in mind.
- **Legally:** the board will wish to consider compliance with data protection provisions, particularly, the confidentiality and security of data.
- **Operationally:** the board will consider the resilience of the service, the supply of service data, and monitoring and review procedures.
- **Financially:** the board will wish to consider unit cost, profit per unit, service credits, and the cost (in time) of dispute escalation processes.

Depending on the complexity of the outsourcing project, typically, these functions will be administered by the retained IT department which, in turn, may be responsible to a project management team which may be accountable to a senior management team (perhaps including the CIO and CTO), and upwards to the board.

Traditionally, this process has been conducted manually. However, in the case of multiple SLAs, the process can easily become cumbersome, costly, labour intensive and prone to dispute. Technology employed to date has

9: Managing the Contract, the SLA and the Transition

included the *ad hoc* use of spreadsheets and Word documents which have done little to simplify the process.

Software is now available to automate the service management process. Oblicore[14] has developed a solution which maps out the management of the portfolio of services and the levels at which they are provided.

The portfolio (or catalogue) of services defines the services to be offered, activates them and defines the standards by which they are to be measured. It is referred to as service portfolio management.

The solution can also be programmed to manage the services levels, establishing the contract, defining relevant measurements, defining reports, setting performance parameters, all in collaboration with the supplier.

The benefits are significant. The process is standardised and the data-gathering process is more consistent. Different metrics can be applied without difficulty, for example, performance, usage or financial metrics. The infrastructure allows oversight network monitoring of all types of application and enables instant comparisons to be made with past performance.

Audit

No matter how realistic the metrics may be, their effectiveness can only be measured against a properly conducted audit. The audit process is an essential feature of governance – that of transparency – and presents clear

---

[14] www.oblicore.com

9: Managing the Contract, the SLA and the Transition

evidence of compliance, or non-compliance with the contract and SLA.

The audit is also a key risk awareness and risk management process. It can identify trends in performance that may lead to problems further ahead and can recommend controls that address inconsistencies. The potential range of an audit is significant and can stretch from minute examination of detailed metrics, to discrepancies, to investigation into fraudulent activity and even the activity of other management teams.

What are the types of area that the board will wish to audit?

- **Strategically:** the board will wish to check the supplier's continuing performance under the SLA to ensure that the contract as a whole remains on course to meet the organisation's objectives.
- **Technologically:** the board will wish to check the performance of the supplier's systems, applications and infrastructures; and if the contract is for a period of years, the frequency with which they are upgraded.
- **Legally:** the organisation will wish to check the supplier's processes and procedures for maintaining compliance with relevant legal, regulatory and industry codes and evidence of continuing certification under agreed British, European and international standards.
- **Operationally:** the board will wish to check the continuing calibre and capacity of personnel employed by the supplier and their ability to maintain the standards of performance under the SLA, the controls in place and evidence of a continuing risk awareness and management strategy.
- **Financially:** the board will wish to check: the continuing financial ability of the supplier to conform to

9: Managing the Contract, the SLA and the Transition

its financial commitments under the contract and SLA; the costs associated with the SLA; verification of the accounting and reporting processes of the supplier; and the overall continuing financial viability of the contract and SLA against the metrics agreed under the SLA.

The audit may be conducted by the supplier, but, although auditors are bound by professional standards, there is obvious potential for a conflict of interest to arise. Therefore, the board should consider obtaining the services of its own auditors to whom data for the purposes of the audit will be supplied by an audit team, perhaps including the CEO, CTO and CFO, co-opting others (particularly, in-house or external legal advice) as necessary.

SLA relationships

This section is confined to the critical issues to be addressed in managing relationships arising in the development and early implementation of the SLA.

Management of relationships in respect of the SLA must be distinguished from managing the relationships arising and continuing for the several years in an outsourcing project.

Relationships in the early stages of implementing an SLA are a key element in ensuring a successful outcome for both parties. In the context of outsourcing IT, difficulties can arise when the personnel in two organisations, who are otherwise complete strangers to each other, are suddenly required to co-operate in a business project, the success of which may be vital to one or other of them The only approach is to foster a culture through mutual trust and respect through continuous and transparent communication and feedback.

9: Managing the Contract, the SLA and the Transition

A successful relationship depends to a great extent on the organisations creating the correct business framework within which the relationship can thrive. It is for the organisation to drive the progress of the contract.

The organisation should be in control of the process – the supplier is merely responding to the requirements of a customer – and, therefore, the organisation must set the tone for the relationship with the supplier.

The organisation must clearly define and communicate its needs and business objectives to the supplier so as to avoid misunderstandings. Failure to do so will lead to confusion and may ultimately result in disputes.

The retained IT department

Clear, concise and comprehensive contract and SLA documentation providing for all eventualities as practicably as possible will help to minimise ambiguities, uncertainty and disputes, all of which tend to undermine relationships.

The contents and management of the contract and SLA were considered earlier. In terms of relationship management, incentives for exceeding expectations and penalties for substandard performance are of considerable importance.

As part of contract and SLA management, it is important that the levels of management infrastructure concerned with administering the outsourcing project should correspond with each other as far as possible.

An example might be the creation of joint teams to address critical stages of the contract and SLA, with defined scoping of areas of responsibility.

9: Managing the Contract, the SLA and the Transition

A correct management framework will not function effectively without the correct appointments. This will involve identifying personnel with skills and abilities to:

- accept leadership responsibilities and drive the project;
- provide a combination of technical, management, financial and compliance experience and competence;
- oversee and supervise the operation of the project;
- provide relationship management skills, perhaps consultants, capable of liaising effectively with the supplier's management teams; and
- provide dispute resolution skills able to manage any disagreements subject to the escalation process.

Andrea Spiegelhoff[15], EMEA Lead for Service Management and Governance at TPI, suggests that, in deciding the composition of the retained IT department, the organisation needs to consider the following with regards to people and skills:

- What are the considerations, skills and capabilities necessary for effective service management and governance?
- How can an assessment be made of available resource capability and skills?
- How can skills be maintained in the long run?

She explains:

The retained IT department will need business capability in the form of commercial management of the service performance.

It will also need to change behaviourally in as much as the informality of an in-house IT department will be replaced by a

---

[15] Interview: 19 June 2009.

9: Managing the Contract, the SLA and the Transition

relationship with the supplier which will require a formal approach that recognises a professional and commercial relationship.

She suggests that four areas of management skills will be needed if the project is to achieve its objective.

Contract management

This role includes: contract change management; contract compliance management; contract interpretation; issue management and dispute resolution; service provider audit; governance library set-up and maintenance; and third party contracts management.

Finance management

This role includes: invoicing management; service credits application; value assurance management; financial analysis and planning; contract pricing adjustments management; development of transparent chargeback mechanisms and management fees for the retained IT department.

Performance management

This role includes: performance analysis and service delivery management; service requests and authorisation; service level management; security management; architecture and standards management; risk management; asset management; incident management; and escalation procedures.

9: Managing the Contract, the SLA and the Transition

Relationship management

As regards the supplier, this role includes: the ability to form a partnership; clear interfaces during the lifetime of the project; in multi-sourcing projects, the ability to secure service integration from all suppliers; and the need for 'people' skills.

As regards the end-user, the role includes: the need to keep end-users informed; addressing potential innovation; managing end-user demand, addressing stakeholder and shareholder interests; awareness of regulatory issues, communications management and customer satisfaction management.

The importance of the constitution of the retained IT department should not be under-estimated. She explains:

The inability of the retained IT department to manage the project during its lifetime is a common factor in project failure. Often, the organisation overlooks its importance; or decides not to commit the necessary resources fearing an adverse impact on the profitability of the project.

New roles, responsibilities and skills will, therefore, be needed to build expertise for managing suppliers, and may include:

- skills in identifying new or additional IT to meet or anticipate specific customer requirements;
- contract management skills, supported by a suitably trained team;
- SLA management skills, supported by a suitably trained team;
- legal and compliance expertise;
- performance and data analysis skills;

9: Managing the Contract, the SLA and the Transition

- knowledge and understanding of new IT developments and its potential for addition to the organisation's portfolio of outsourced services;
- an IT relationship manager to address the issues arising with the supplier throughout the project.

Every project is different and so the constitution of the retained IT department will be different. Andy McCallum[16] says, 'SHL has a retained IT department comprising an Infrastructure Service Manager, an Application Services Manager and a Workplace Services Manager, who are headed up by the Service Delivery Director'.

The Cloud model

In the Cloud model, the retained IT department will also require different skills and a different type of leadership. These skills relate less to IT facilities, and rather to IT management. They will involve: liaising with senior management; overseeing the introduction of any changes arising from the Cloud model; ensuring personnel have the appropriate skills to manage the relationship with the supplier and ensuring personnel participate in the new arrangements.

Cloud technology presents a challenge to the management of IT, in as much as management of the Cloud model will only be considered successful once the Cloud model itself can be seen to offer benefits to the organisation and value to its customers.

---

[16] Interview: 23 June 2009

9: Managing the Contract, the SLA and the Transition

These are simply examples of how an 'IT' department may be reconstituted after an outsourcing contract takes effect. The nature of the IT function changes from operational to managerial. More managerial functions may be needed according to the extent of the outsourcing, particularly where multiple suppliers are involved.

The roles vary considerably in nature. Clear leadership skills will be needed to harness the new team and ensure that it is motivated to operate on the governance principles adopted by the organisation.

An assessment will need to be made as to the extent to which the functions of the reconstituted IT department might overlap or impinge upon those of the project management team and how this can be managed.

It is clear to see that, in offloading what the organisation might regard as a burdensome costly and complex function to a third party, the replacement is likely to require adroit and competent management skills, supported, where necessary, with suitable training.

Knowing the supplier

The organisation should gain as much knowledge as possible about the contracted supplier and any personnel to be employed by the supplier for performance of the contract in the pre-contract phase. The organisation must satisfy itself that the supplier is trustworthy, dependable and is sympathetic to the business objectives of the organisation in embarking on an outsourcing strategy. In particular, the organisation must be satisfied, as far as possible, that the supplier's personnel will respect any confidentiality required by the contract.

9: Managing the Contract, the SLA and the Transition

As part of this process, it is important to identify at the earliest possible stage, the potential for personality conflicts arising within the management infrastructure.

Managing people

While researching the potential relationship with a supplier, the organisation must not overlook the relationship with its own employees who may be involved in the project. They may be personnel who will be transferred under the contract; they may be potential redundancies; or they may be personnel who are displaced or redeployed after the outsourcing project has been implemented.

Standard and well-recognised management strategies can assist in the process:

- continuous, clear and timely communication with all relevant personnel at all levels from top management;
- provision of relevant information at regular intervals; and
- establishment of panels of representatives to give feedback and resolve complaints.

The importance of managing personnel is that for the project to succeed there must be an organisation-wide understanding of the implications and reasonable expectations of the project, if the necessary level of support is to be obtained.

The wider issues to be addressed concerning the management of personnel throughout the project are considered within the context of managing operational risks and are considered later.

9: Managing the Contract, the SLA and the Transition

Transition

The transition stage begins immediately steps are taken to implement the contract and SLA and ends with a formal sign-off in respect of all outstanding issues. The transition period should be as brief as reasonably possible, as long transition periods can result in the project losing impetus.

In the early days of the contract, a smooth transition is imperative. The principal aim of the organisation should be to: ensure a seamless handover which will pass unnoticed by customers; build up trust with the supplier for long-term success; address any problems promptly and decisively; and set down firm and practical working procedures, for example, over reporting and billing.

Problems that frequently arise, through having been overlooked, include:

- incomplete disclosure;
- misunderstandings;
- lack of consultation;
- inadequate planning;
- disruptive changes of, and for, personnel; and
- inadequate change processes.

The transition stage needs to be managed either by a suitable skilled internal team, or a specialist external team.

The proposals of prospective suppliers on the key features for managing the transition stage may be raised during the tendering process. The transition may involve:

- outsourcing a large number of personnel; or
- retraining or recruiting personnel for the retained department to manage the contract and SLA.

9: Managing the Contract, the SLA and the Transition

Transition is effectively a project in itself and should, therefore, involve a project manager. Some organisations hire a transition manager but their specialist expertise can involve significant expense. If a transition manager is appointed, a sensible strategy is to ensure that this is mirrored by a correspondingly assembled team by the supplier.

Some suppliers include transition management as part of the outsourcing service. While this may be a welcome solution to an inexperienced organisation, the risk is that, with the need for profit as its primary objective, the supplier may employ poorly skilled personnel which, in turn, may result in inadequate management of the process, or even jeopardise the project itself.

If the transition is to be treated as a project, it must be managed in the same way as a project. This may involve:

- appointment of a team with the required skills;
- a schedule of key stages and their timing;
- a schedule of required resources;
- a schedule of required service levels;
- specified monitoring processes;
- specified reporting responsibilities; and
- specified dispute resolution processes.

Fundamentally, a successful transition is founded upon the satisfactory management of the relationship with the supplier. The appointment of a project manager – or transition manager – with relationship skills is likely to be critical to the effectiveness of the transition.

During the transition period, the concerns of stakeholders and end-users should not be neglected. It may not be necessary to have these interests specifically represented on

9: Managing the Contract, the SLA and the Transition

the transition team, but if they are not, the transition team should develop clear lines of communication to ensure those concerned – and any other parties with legitimate concerns – are sufficiently informed as the transition process proceeds.

CHAPTER 10: CONTRACT CHANGE CONTROL

An outsourcing contract may remain effective for several years. Over such a long period, it is inevitable that changes will be needed to ensure that the contract reflects both parties' intentions during the currency of the project. It is important that mechanisms are included in the contract that provide for changes to take place through a properly managed process.

Reasons for change

In such a fast moving industry as IT, a wide variety of changes need to be addressed. New hardware and software developments, emerging markets, new business environments, changing user needs and new suppliers are just some of the circumstances which may necessitate change to an outsourcing contract. Simply maintaining the currency of the contract may require changes.

Business environments can change rapidly. A supplier may develop the capability of providing more sophisticated solutions, greater processing, or larger storage facilities.

An end-user may wish to widen business goals and objectives to meet a more competitive marketplace.

An organisation may wish to restructure with a view to competing in global markets, or may be required to comply with regulatory issues which the contract does not address.

10: Contract Change Control

Types of change

There are two principal types of change:

- change within the contract itself agreed by the parties; and
- change to the contract necessitated by circumstances.

The first may take the form of: an agreed amendment in the shape of a new term or condition of the contract which may be formally amended; or changes to the manner of performance of an existing term (for example, a change in service levels); or an agreed change to the way in which a term of the contract is to be construed.

The second arises from external events bringing pressure to bear on the parties to amend the contract. Typical examples include:

- new developments in trade and industry;
- a requirement by the organisation for the supplier to undertake research and development services;
- advances in technology;
- demands by end-users for new services for which an existing outsourcing contract makes no provision;
- new legal, regulatory and compliance provisions that were not contemplated when the contract was originally made;
- a decision by the organisation to pursue new business strategies that were not contemplated by the contract.

The contract should be flexible enough to allow for change without undue difficulty. To some extent, depending on the nature of the contracted services, some variations may be anticipated, such as slight changes in service performance, or the anticipation of future requirements.

10: Contract Change Control

Whatever the change proposed, consideration should be given as to its viability and practicality. It is important to avoid the potential for a single, relatively minor change requiring a series of amendments throughout the main contract and even its schedules.

Considerations

Unless the contract provides otherwise, changes may be made by either party. In general terms, both parties should decide whether the change is necessary and assign it a degree of priority.

A careful assessment of the implications of the change needs to be made. Typical questions to ask include: whether the change is in line with the original business objectives of the outsourcing project; the cost implications; the anticipated benefits; and the importance of the proposed change.

However, circumstances may enforce change – most commonly for legal or compliance reasons – in which case, the change should be introduced with the minimum of delay.

Administration

If a change is agreed in principle between the parties, steps should be taken to ensure there is no misunderstanding and that it is fully and mutually understood. Further, any change to the contract should be adequately recorded to avoid disputes at a later stage.

A formal procedure should be adopted to ensure that the various considerations of the parties receive due attention.

10: Contract Change Control

The following steps are suggested:

- **Step one:** submission of a costed proposal, with timescales and reasons to the supplier.
- **Step two:** documented consideration of the impact of the proposed change on all other aspects of the contract and schedules.
- **Step three:** meeting with the supplier to consider the proposal and any amendments.
- **Step four:** if agreement cannot be reached, or if the supplier refuses the proposal, consideration of whether an escalation process should be implemented.
- **Step five:** if agreement is reached, a draft of the amendment should be agreed between the parties, together with a date for implementation and effect.
- **Step six:** provision should be made for the amendment to be recorded so as to enable future reference to be made, possibly several years later.

Every organisation will have a preferred management structure. On the basis, however, that almost all organisations will assemble a project management team for managing an outsourcing project, it is this team that is likely to be most effective in controlling changes. The project team will know the issues and have most experience of what is required. If needs be, external assistance can be obtained, either from consultants or from other expertise within the organisation.

Change control is a subset of contract and SLA management. Without effective mechanisms for managing change during the contract term, there is a danger that the project may be derailed. Flexibility and a willingness to adapt to change is a key requirement, if the parties intend to benefit from the project.

CHAPTER 11: CONTRACT EXIT

Managing the termination of an outsourcing contract requires a number of complex issues to be addressed if a good relationship with the supplier is to be maintained throughout and after the process. The outsourcing process should not be indefinite as circumstances change and contracts need adjustment to reflect the parties' circumstances and interests.

The contract term

An outsourcing contract may be:

- for a fixed term; or
- for a continuous period, renewable or terminable at certain agreed intervals upon agreed notice.

A contract may be terminated by mutual agreement with an agreed period of notice; unilaterally by either party upon notice in accordance with the provisions of the contract, for example, for breach of contract for persistent failure to maintain service levels; or by natural expiry.

The contract needs to provide for the different situations in which either party might wish to serve notice during the project. It is important that this process is considered during the contract negotiations, however difficult it may be to envisage future circumstances.

In particular, the length of the contract requires careful thought. Typically, contracts may vary from periods of two to five years or even longer. Long contracts facilitate a more secure relationship and provide for continuity and

11: Contract Exit

indicate commitment. However, they can narrow the organisation's options, stifle innovation and lead to undue complacency on the part of the supplier.

Reasons for termination can be various. Contracts ended by mutual agreement may provide for payment of a fee or some measure of compensation. Other reasons include: insolvency; breach of contract; winding-up; merger and acquisition; *force majeure* (greater force); and changed business strategies.

From the organisation's perspective, it is desirable that the supplier's right to terminate is limited as far as possible, because receipt of notice from a supplier may leave the organisation in an exposed and vulnerable position.

Exit options

At the end of the contract, the organisation has certain options, the organisation may:

- renew the contract with the supplier for a further period;
- re-tender for outsourcing services; or
- simply terminate the relationship with the supplier and take the service in house.

Renewal for a further period

Renewal of the contract may require some relatively straightforward amendments to the expired contract to reflect the fresh needs of the parties. Any changes must be introduced by agreement.

The organisation may consider incentives for the supplier to continue with a further agreement by broadening the

11: Contract Exit

service provision required under the contract as a condition of its extension. Thought should be given to the same considerations that arise when negotiating and agreeing the terms and processes of the original contract, so that no important provisions are overlooked.

Re-tendering for new services

If the organisation decides to re-tender, the process of identifying a new supplier will be repeated in terms of the:

- selection of an outsourcing strategy;
- selection of an outsourcing supplier;
- tendering and negotiations to contract;
- contract terms and documentation;
- SLA;
- operational plans for managing the contract;
- post-contract change controls; and
- termination of the contract (exit).

The organisation may decide to include the original supplier in the tendering process. It is important that there should be equal competition between potential suppliers, so that the organisation can reach an objective decision when selecting a supplier and also maintain a good relationship with the supplier.

For the purposes of preparing the re-tendering documentation, the organisation will require certain information from the supplier in connection with its operations under the original contract. So the organisation can identify any assets to be included in the new contract, schedules should be provided that identify:

11: Contract Exit

- **Assets:** primarily hardware and software, but also any specific assets relevant to the outsourcing.
- **Documents:** these might include: contracts and schedules; SLAs; licences; data protection contracts; and any other documentation relating to performance of the outsourcing function.
- **Personnel issues:** a schedule of employees' contracts, records and any relevant TUPE 2006 documentation.
- **Financial issues:** details of all relevant financial records relating to the performance of the outsourcing function, such as details of contracts the supplier has with third parties, for example, for the disposal of equipment.

The sensitive and confidential nature of this information will warrant an NDA between the outgoing and any new supplier.

The question of any staff transfers involved under the original outsourcing contract will need to be addressed. The organisation may wish to consider re-engaging certain personnel transferred under the original contract. If so, compliance issues may arise under TUPE 2006 and the DPA, as well as issues of confidentiality.

The organisation should check that, in any re-assignment of staff at the termination of an outsourcing contract, the team has substantially the same skills and qualifications as that transferred under the original contract and that the supplier has not 'diluted' the competence of the team with poor quality staff.

A re-tendering exercise is not a decision to be taken lightly. It will involve forging a relationship with new suppliers and consequent expense and disruption to the organisation and any personnel involved.

11: Contract Exit

Termination of the relationship

Where the organisation decides to terminate the contract and does not propose to re-tender, the supplier must be requested to supply full details of the resources used for the supply of its services.

The organisation will need immediate access to all assets and relevant personnel and any premises to enable its business to operate normally.

Relevant contracts, leases and licences for the use of any equipment, software and any other resources must be identified, so that they can be considered for transfer to, or purchase by, the organisation, or re-assignment to another party, or some other form of disposal.

Thought will need to be given to the implications of acquiring any shared assets and, generally, to the financial viability of acquiring the supplier's entire stock of assets.

Particular care will need to be given to the disposal of any assets that involve intellectual property, for example, copyright documentation, such as performance logs. Software licences will need to be re-assigned, but the situation regarding modified software is more problematic.

Bespoke software created by the supplier for the purposes of the original contract may end up with a third-party competitor and there may be a dispute over the intellectual property rights in the software.

Consideration must also be given to any intellectual property rights in data used in supplying the services and any know-how acquired by the supplier during the provision of the services.

11: Contract Exit

The contract should include an obligation on the part of the supplier to provide all additional assistance that is reasonably required by the organisation from time to time in connection with the termination process. This is important particularly where relations may have become embittered before or during the termination process.

Managing the exit strategy

The complexities of handling an exit strategy dictate the need for careful planning. This should address the need for transfer of the services to the organisation in house, or to another supplier.

Typical issues to consider include:

- a schedule of processes and procedures for managing the transition;
- a schedule of personnel to be involved together with their respective roles and responsibilities;
- a timetable and event plan;
- the identification of any resources needed to manage the strategy;
- a plan for promulgation of the procedure and communication with staff;
- a schedule for addressing the transfer of assets;
- a schedule for the transfer of any personnel;
- a schedule for the management of software and intellectual property rights; and
- a schedule of the costs involved.

11: Contract Exit

Disputes

The contract provides for appropriate notices to be given to address the various exit options discussed earlier.

There may also be occasions where the contract is brought to an end without the wish of either party. In a situation where an event occurs that makes the contract impossible to fulfil – referred to as frustration of contract in legal jargon – it may be brought to an end. A *force majeure* clause commonly addresses this situation in outsourcing contracts.

Contract terms

Situations may arise where parties are in dispute and resort to legal remedies. Most frequently, a breach of a contract term may be alleged. This may be a:

- breach of condition; or
- breach of warranty.

A condition is a provision of fundamental importance such that any breach may entitle the other party to repudiate the contract and claim damages.

A warranty relates to issues of less fundamental importance and any breach may entitle the other party to damages only.

A third type of provision to address disputes is an indemnity, when one party agrees to indemnify the other against financial loss arising from specific circumstances.

A fourth mechanism of resort is the limitation of liability, where one party may try to limit its liability to the other in certain circumstances. The courts will not uphold attempts to limit total liability in commercial contracts because the courts consider them unreasonable and will generally look

11: Contract Exit

to the reasonableness of any term of the contract that seeks to exclude liability.

In outsourcing contracts, a supplier may try to limit its liability to a certain sum, in which event the organisation must ensure that the supplier takes out insurance cover in respect of any claim that may exceed the cover.

Remedies

Claims by one party against another in an outsourcing project may typically arise where one party alleges against the other:

- negligence in the performance of the contract;
- negligent mis-statement on which the other party relied to its detriment;
- misuse of software, for example, a breach of the software licence; or
- infringement of intellectual property rights.

Each outsourcing project is different and so a wide range of activities may fall into the general category of a breach of contract. Each situation must be considered individually.

If the breach is fundamental, the court may allow the injured party to repudiate the contract and claim damages. Alternatively, the court may decide that damages alone are sufficient remedy.

There are two forms of damages – general damages which are a recompense for unquantifiable losses, such as inconvenience and general loss to the organisation arising from the breach – and special damages which relate to specific quantifiable losses. In each case, the aim is to

11: Contract Exit

return the injured party to a position as though the breach had not occurred.

In certain cases, a court may also order an injunction to prevent an alleged breach of contract from continuing. A typical example of the use of this remedy would be for the unauthorised copying of software under the CDPA.

In the courts of England and Wales, strict periods of limitation apply to the bringing of different types of legal proceedings, which if not launched within the period specified by law, may prevent an injured party from obtaining any remedy from the courts.

Therefore, whenever legal proceedings are contemplated, specialist legal advice should always be sought immediately and in any event, as soon as possible after the alleged breach.

Dispute resolution

Outsourcing contracts may be of several years' duration, during which it is quite possible that issues and problems will arise between the parties. Areas for potential dispute are many and various. Examples include: issues over service quality and pricing mechanisms; misalignment of the project with the organisation's objectives; end-user dissatisfaction; personality conflicts; and a supplier losing the confidence of the organisation.

The contract and SLA reflect the agreement between the parties and should be the first point of reference in the event of a dispute. The contract documentation may offer a solution by providing for remedies that address the problem, for example:

11: Contract Exit

- service credits for poor performance;
- withholding payment for poor performance;
- rights for the organisation to step in and take over the project;
- rights for the organisation to conduct an audit.

Escalation

A key principle of corporate governance is that the board of directors should establish lines of responsibility and accountability and this applies to dispute management.

The board should establish processes and procedures within the SLA for the management of disputes that are relatively minor, but which may escalate and significantly affect the performance of the contract, and the parties' relationship, if not addressed.

The most common procedure is for meetings to occur on a regular basis between representatives of the organisation and counterparts from the supplier. In the initial stages, selected members of the parties' respective project teams are likely to be most appropriate, depending on the nature of the dispute.

If the dispute cannot be resolved at this level, an escalation process follows in which the issue is referred to correspondingly senior levels of the parties' management. In this respect, it is sensible for the board to give some thought at the outset of the personnel whom it identifies as likely to be most competent for this purpose.

Each problem should be formally documented and recorded, identifying personnel responsible for resolution; and the path of the escalation process should be auditable.

11: Contract Exit

Minutes of successive attempts to resolve the problem should be recorded for reference at a later date, if necessary by more senior management teams.

The board should ensure that the escalation team has a clear idea of the objective of achieving a solution. Objectives may include: performance improvement; alteration to service provision; the return of confidence in the relationship; resolution of end-user issues; or even termination of the contract.

It is also important that the parties are agreed on the facts, or, if there is disagreement, the issues in dispute are clear. Establishing the facts may not be that easy and it may be necessary to refer to minutes of previous meetings and discussions with relevant personnel before an assessment of the organisation's position is clear. Documents and communications exchanged between the parties should also be examined.

There are various solutions that can emerge from the escalation process, which is generally informal and flexible. Solutions include:

- termination of the contract by agreement;
- changes to the contract or SLA;
- changes of personnel (for example, in personality conflicts);
- financial compensation; and
- step-in by the organisation – where the organisation assumes management of the contract in place of the supplier, but in practical terms this is difficult to achieve if the relationship with the supplier is to survive.

Escalation processes highlight a key issue which threads through all aspects of an outsourcing project. As far as

11: Contract Exit

possible, the board should ensure that the management structure of the supplier mirrors that of the organisation. In this way, an individual in the organisation wishing to raise any issue with the supplier should have a counterpart to approach in the first instance.

Most contracts will contain a provision for further stages of any unresolved dispute to be referred for formal dispute resolution processes. There are two types of process employed for this purpose.

Alternative dispute resolution (ADR)

This is used to include various mediation processes for resolving disputes. The underlying principle of mediation is that its approach is conciliatory; the concept of fault is absent and the parties meet under the auspices of a professional mediator to try to devise a solution to the problem that addresses their respective concerns. ADR is quicker and usually less expensive than court proceedings.

Arbitration

Arbitration is more formal than ADR and is governed by the Arbitration Act 1996. Like court proceedings, it is adversarial rather than conciliatory but is less formal, although not necessarily less expensive because a formal hearing is involved where parties are legally represented. The parties argue their case before an arbitrator professionally qualified in the area of dispute concerned.

11: Contract Exit

Back-sourcing

The termination of an outsourcing agreement by an organisation may indicate that the organisation has decided to bring the outsourced services back in house. Usually there is a combination of reasons.

Reaching a decision

There may be a number of operational reasons for this decision.

- The perceived economies of scale and the effort in managing the outsourcing process, for example, obtaining multiple software licences, might have been equally achievable if the processes had been performed by an in-house IT department.
- Some of the savings that the supplier offered might have been achievable by a more efficiently managed IT department.
- Persistent disputes may have arisen from an inadequately drawn contract.
- The organisation may have overlooked, or failed to realise that, the cost of outsourcing is directly related to the quality of the services and that demands for greater quality result in higher supplier costs.
- The organisation may have felt dissatisfaction with the quality of the supplier's services; combined with a general sense that the operation is not as efficient, cost-effective, or manageable as expected, and that in terms of the management and administrative changes occasioned by the project involved, the function could just as satisfactorily be managed in house.

11: Contract Exit

- At the end of the contract, the organisation may have grown and its additional requirements and outsourcing may be less cost-effective.
- There may also be strategic reasons. There may have been a merger or acquisition, so that the supplier's services become unnecessary.
- The business goals of the organisation may have changed, so that the supplier's services become less relevant.

On the other hand, in certain circumstances it may not be cost-effective to back-source. For instance, back-sourcing an entire IT infrastructure might be prohibitive if it entailed hiring and training an entire workforce – possibly making redundant the personnel in the retained IT department.

The process of virtualisation means that many organisations contemplating outsourcing IT now have considerable computing power at their disposal in house and the incentive to outsource diminishes.

A helpful method of arriving at a decision to back-source and in-source is to identify of the cost of providing the outsourced services in house and to make a comparison with the total of the supplier's cost, the cost of establishing an in-house provision, and the cost of disbanding or retraining the retained IT department.

Managing the process

The integral role that IT plays in almost every aspect of any organisation means that a poorly managed and administered back-sourcing strategy may result in adverse operational effects, for instance, downtime, or damage to partner or customer relationships.

11: Contract Exit

A back-sourcing strategy should, therefore, be carefully planned. It is arguable that the implications of back-sourcing should be considered at the pre-contract stage of the outsourcing project. This will enable the organisation to plan at least some provision for the end of the project. For example, if an entire IT department needs to be reconstructed, considerable time, effort, expense and resources will be needed to represent top-level commitment.

If the outsourcing project has run for a number of years, a new IT infrastructure may need to be constructed.

Steps must be taken to ensure the project proceeds in an orderly way.

The board, supported by an executive or project management team, perhaps also with consultancy, and certainly with legal, assistance, must identify all services, assets and personnel included in the original outsourcing contract. A decision must then be reached over which of the original outsourced functions are to be performed in house.

The success of a back-sourcing project lies in obtaining the co-operation of the original supplier. The original outsourcing contract should stipulate that the supplier will assist should back-sourcing be necessary.

A back-sourcing project is an outsourcing project in reverse and should, therefore, be characterised by the same features. Project management is considered in detail later, but typical features will include agreement on: the stages of the project; a suitable timetable; issue escalation procedures; and monitoring and reporting processes.

11: Contract Exit

Transition in back-sourcing

A smooth transition is essential for ensuring the operational continuity of services to the organisation's customers and for maintaining relationships with others involved in the services that are being back-sourced.

If there is to be a split between those services to be back-sourced and those which are to remain outsourced, there must be a clear agreement with the supplier and an appropriate amendment to the outsourcing contract.

It is sensible to devise a structured plan which establishes how the transition process is to be managed. The primary issues to be addressed fall in the categories of service provision, technology and communications.

The principles of transition under an outsourcing contract and SLA were considered earlier. An organisation must recognise that back-sourcing is just as much a project as outsourcing.

A suitably qualified team should be assembled under the supervision of a project manager and IT manager with relevant experience of performing and managing the process of back-sourcing the IT function. If possible and practical, a similar team should be assembled by the supplier throughout the process.

It is important to remember that there are stakeholder interests in the success of a back-sourcing project. These include not only the board, but also executives, personnel, strategic and operational allies and business partners, and end-users. Consideration should be given either to affording some element of representation on the team for these interests, or ensuring that channels of communication are available for exchange of dialogue.

11: Contract Exit

Service provision

In order to maintain continuity of service standards, the organisation must ensure that, as far as possible, it is equipped with all necessary personnel, assets and IT hardware and software.

An audit should be conducted of each of these three categories, so that the organisation can assess which are to be reassigned by the supplier, which it already possesses and which must be acquired.

The agreement with the supplier should provide for support until the back-sourcing project is complete.

Technology

As confidential data in the possession of the supplier is now being reassigned to the organisation, steps should be taken to ensure that appropriate security policies and processes are adopted to comply with data protection principles.

As a further data protection measure, steps should be taken to prepare and implement a disaster recovery and business continuity plan to take account of the 'new' services that the organisation will now be undertaking.

Communications

It is essential for the continuity of operations that all concerned in the process are kept informed regularly. They will include:

- personnel to be reassigned to the organisation;
- affected personnel within the organisation;
- the organisation's affected customers;

11: Contract Exit

- stakeholders, such as introducers or referrers of work;
- shareholders;
- industry partners; and
- investors.

It is particularly important that all personnel concerned have a clear understanding of their new roles and responsibilities once the back-sourced arrangements are completed. In some cases, provision may need to be made for further skills training, particularly if new IT is to be acquired.

Back-sourcing is not necessarily an easy option. In some cases, the implementation process may be almost as complex as the original outsourcing project. Careful planning and the deployment of the necessary resources are paramount for a successful back-sourcing project.

CHAPTER 12: CORPORATE GOVERNANCE

IT plays a pivotal role in the performance of almost every organisation. Without IT, most organisations could hardly function to any level of performance acceptable to its customers, shareholders or stakeholders.

A decision to develop and implement a strategy that involves the outsourcing of an organisation's IT resources, therefore, goes to the core of its ability to perform and compete. Such a strategy has fundamental implications for customers, shareholders and stakeholders, particularly its personnel.

Outsourcing IT involves a profound change in the manner in which an organisation applies its resources in the achievement of its business objectives. The organisation is entrusting a major resource for the delivery of its products and services to customers to a third-party supplier with which it may be quite unfamiliar.

It follows that, in developing and implementing such a strategy, sound corporate and business principles must be applied. In every corporate body, the responsibility for identification, development and execution of a strategy lies with the board of directors. It is, therefore, the board of directors who must lead the way in observing and applying sound principles. It is the board of directors that decides the nature of a strategy, defines its scope, and declares and oversees the areas of responsibility for its execution.

In deciding its strategy, the board must be transparent in its decision-making processes, promulgating decisions to its stakeholders, shareholders and customers, because it is to

12: Corporate Governance

these bodies that the board is accountable. The board must address two further issues associated with this process: legal and regulatory compliance and risk management.

The fulfilment of these obligations applies as much to outsourcing the IT function as any other company business. An IT outsourcing project is especially critical to the organisation's viability because of the vital importance of IT as a resource for its performance against its competitors.

The outsourcing process has been examined in previous chapters. It is highly complex. There is considerable scope for an organisation to sustain significant loss or damage to its business performance, profitability, competitiveness and reputation in the marketplace, quite apart from the threat of proceedings for legal and regulatory non-compliance, if the project is not properly managed.

Governance establishes sound business principles that begin at board level. These principles set levels of conduct that underpin the quality of its decision-making. Their observation and application are of critical importance in an IT outsourcing project.

This chapter considers the general concept of corporate governance and identifies the general implications for boards of directors in conducting company business. The next chapter examines a subset of corporate governance, IT governance, and its impact on outsourcing the IT function. Following that, a further subset, project governance, is considered in the context of outsourcing IT.

The process of implementing an IT outsourcing project is complex and requires significant managerial skills and capability at all levels of an organisation. Such management

12: Corporate Governance

must be founded upon a relevant and comprehensive governance infrastructure.

What is governance? The Shorter Edition of the Oxford English Dictionary (2002) includes a reference to governance as '... the action, manner or fact of governing, government: controlling, regulating influence; control, mastery, the state of being governed; good order...' Successful management of outsourcing the IT function requires risks to be managed adequately, and the project to be directed and managed within a framework that will ensure it achieves its business objectives.

Definition

A universally comprehensive definition of corporate governance is elusive because each organisation is different and functions in different ways.

On 1 December 1992, the Cadbury Report[17] was published which included a 'code of best practice designed to achieve the necessary high standards of corporate behaviour'.

In practical terms, this represents the methods by which a board of directors controls and manages the performance of an organisation, meeting the interests of shareholders who appoint them, satisfying the requirements of auditors, setting strategy, driving implementation through executive supervision, and ensuring regulatory compliance and effective risk management.

---

[17] *The Financial Aspects of Corporate Governance,* December 1992, available at: www.ecgi.org/codes/documents/cadbury.pdf.

12: Corporate Governance

This is achieved by well-defined lines of responsibility and accountability at all levels of the organisation underpinned by a transparent decision-making process.

In 2004, the OECD[18] established twelve principles of corporate governance comprising six principles, and six guideline annotations. Broadly, they can be summarised as follows:

- the promotion of transparent and effective markets consistent with the rule of law, identifying responsibilities among supervisory, regulatory and enforcement authorities;
- the protection of shareholders;
- the equitable treatment of shareholders;
- recognition of the rights of shareholders and the encouragement of co-operation between corporations and stakeholders to ensure a sound financial enterprise;
- timely and accurate disclosure of all material matters;
- board monitoring of management and board accountability to the company and shareholders.

A simple summary is that of Alan Calder:[19] 'The holy trinity of good corporate governance has long been seen as shareholder rights, transparency and board accountability'.

The implications of corporate governance are that directors must ensure their decision-making processes are transparent and take account of shareholders' interests in all the organisation's dealings. This extends to all aspects of risk management, including an obligation to have regard for the

---

[18] *OECD Principles of Corporate Governance*, OECD, 2004, available at: www.oecd.org/daf/corporateaffairs/principles/text.

[19] *Corporate Governance*, Calder A, Kogan Page, 2008.

12: Corporate Governance

organisation's profitable performance. These obligations are underpinned by the directors' responsibility and accountability to all stakeholders in the organisation.

Corporate governance frameworks

There are two types of corporate governance framework: the statutory framework and the non-statutory framework

Statutory framework

Corporate governance, as the expression implies, applies to incorporated organisations. Corporate governance principles can also apply to partnerships but the principles are most frequently considered in the context of limited companies.

The statutory framework is founded primarily on a succession of Companies Acts from 1948 through a number of amending and consolidating provisions – including the Companies (Audit, Investigations and Community Enterprise) Act 2004 – up to the Companies Act 2006.

The Companies Act 2006 was implemented as a review and update to address new developments in the corporate sector since the previous legislation, the Companies Act 1985. It provides for each company to have: a memorandum which governs its external functions, including it objects; and articles of association which govern its internal functions, including, directors, shares, meetings and voting rights.

Before the Companies Act 2006, a company was legally bound to confine itself to the object of the memorandum. Any activity beyond the objectives was known legally as *ultra vires* (beyond the powers) in which case directors

12: Corporate Governance

might find themselves personally liable to third parties for any loss. However, under the Companies Act 2006, company objects do not need to be stated.

Directors' duties are enshrined in sections 171-177 of the Companies Act 2006 and, in summary, are to:

- act within their powers;
- promote the success of the company;
- exercise reasonable judgement;
- exercise reasonable care and diligence;
- avoid conflict of interest;
- decline benefits from third parties; and
- declare any interest in transactions and arrangements.

The Companies (Model Articles) Regulations 2008, schedule 1, prescribes the model articles of association for private companies after 1 October 2009. Part 2 of this schedule defines: directors' powers and responsibilities, their decision-making processes and their appointment. Schedules 1, 2 and 3 prescribe model articles for private and public companies.

Corporate governance concerns the relationship between the company and other stakeholders. These include: shareholders and investors; the board of directors; management; personnel; customers; suppliers; creditors; debtors; regulators; and the public.

The common themes of corporate governance are accountability, responsibility, transparency, sound economics and the welfare of shareholders.

Corporate governance has developed an increasingly high profile since the high profile collapses of a number of major organisations in the corporate sector.

12: Corporate Governance

Non-statutory framework

The Cadbury Code, published in 1992, laid the foundation for non-statutory corporate governance. The Combined Code on Corporate Governance was first published in 1998. The latest version of the Combined Code was published in June 2008[20] and applies to all accounting periods beginning on or after 29 June 2008. In its preamble, the Combined Code states: 'Good corporate governance should contribute to better company performance by helping a board discharge its duties in the best interests of shareholders...'

The Combined Code identifies key principles which include the need for: clear lines of responsibility; performance assessments; realistic commercial assessments; adequate controls; transparent reporting; consideration of shareholders; and a clear governance infrastructure.

Companies governed by the Listing Rules of the London Stock Exchange are required to comply with the Combined Code and to include a statement of compliance in each annual report.

Companies listed on AIM in the UK are not strictly required to comply with the Combined Code but the Quoted Companies Alliance published Corporate Governance Guidelines for AIM Companies in February 2007, with a view to helping AIM quoted companies in developing simpler and more manageable corporate governance frameworks in order to promote and encourage a culture of corporate governance.

---

[20] *The Combined Code on Corporate Governance 2008*, available at: www.frc.org.uk.

12: Corporate Governance

Underpinning the all-embracing infrastructure of corporate governance are two frameworks which are critical for the successful management of outsourcing the IT function.

The first is an IT governance framework which prescribes governance principles for the proper management and operation of IT systems and networks by the board, so that IT is integrated within the business.

The second is a project governance framework which prescribes governance principles for the proper management of projects.

CHAPTER 13: IT GOVERNANCE

Numerous reasons are expressed for the failure of outsourcing projects. They include:

- failure of communication between the parties resulting in uncoordinated and misaligned processes;
- poor relationships between the parties at the outset;
- inadequate capabilities of retained IT functions; and
- inadequate governance and management frameworks supporting the project.

A survey for the IT Governance Global Status Report 2008[21] made a number of key findings in respect of the adoption of and attitudes towards IT governance. These included:

- IT governance is still very much a CIO/IT director issue and few non-IT people in the sample had a much more positive view of IT than the IT professionals themselves;
- the importance of IT continues to rise;
- there is still substantial room for improvement in alignment between IT governance and corporate governance – as well as for IT strategy and business strategy;
- good IT governance practices are known and applied but not universally;

---

[21] Source: *IT Governance Global Status Report 2008*, ©2008 IT Governance Institute. All rights reserved. Used by permission.

13: IT Governance

- organisations know who can help them implement IT governance, but appreciation for the available expertise and delivery capability is only average.

These mixed findings suggest that in many organisations, there is a relatively widespread ignorance, at most levels, of the business importance of IT governance.

Definition

Corporate governance is the responsibility of the board: setting strategic objectives; providing leadership; managing executive performance (including risk); and reporting and accounting to shareholders.

IT governance is a 'framework for the leadership, organisational structure and business processes, standards and compliance with these standards'.[22] The aim is to guarantee that the IT function remains aligned with the organisation's strategic objectives.

Criteria

The decision to outsource all or part of the IT function of an organisation is a strategic decision for the board to be reached in accordance with the principles of IT governance. The actual implementation of an outsourcing project is an operational issue (although strategic issues may arise), and is the subject of project governance which is considered in the next chapter.

---

[22] *Corporate Governance*, Calder A, Kogan Page, 2008.

13: IT Governance

While observing and implementing corporate governance principles is a fundamental requirement, this requires the support of specific governance frameworks to address particular functions.

The organisation must include in its governance framework support for external investment in IT, particularly where, as in the case of an outsourcing project, the investment is likely to be over a period of several years.

It cannot be over-emphasised that, throughout its life, an IT outsourcing project must remain aligned with the business goals and objectives of the organisation (and supplier). Both organisation and supplier should approach an IT outsourcing project with IT governance principles in mind and strive to apply them for the duration of the project.

Mutual adoption of IT governance principles aims to bring the parties together in joint management of the relationship. As the relationship begins with the outsourcing contract, the IT governance framework should be introduced at the earliest possible stage and be included within the contract to cover both the transition and subsequent implementation of the contract.

This presents a number of benefits:

- recognised decision-making and accountability hierarchies;
- clear definition of roles and responsibilities, supported by standards, methodologies, policies and protocols;
- a balanced relationship without undue influence exercised by either party;
- long-term commitment and involvement of board and senior management.

13: IT Governance

The board's concern will be to ensure that the strategy is promulgated throughout the organisation and that an appropriate management and operational infrastructure is in place to ensure that it is implemented to achieve the required standard of performance.

The criteria for adopting IT governance principles are widely recognised as:

- the need to adopt and comply with corporate governance principles;
- the need for a framework that will protect information and (electronic) intellectual property;
- the need for a framework that will manage IT risk – such as security and business continuity; and
- the need to develop a competitive edge by cost-effective and efficient execution of the organisation's strategy, as set out by the board.

Therefore, in reaching a strategic decision to outsource, the board must apply corporate governance principles, identifying: the business function it intends IT to perform within the organisation; the specific functions for which it is to be deployed; and the investment it needs to make in IT in order to achieve these objectives.

The board must then identify a framework that will: protect its information and intellectual property; address security and business continuity risks; and ensure the strategy is implemented, so that the organisation's business objectives are achieved.

13: IT Governance

Governance frameworks

Alan Calder[23] suggests that designing an IT governance framework involves eight key decision areas:

- IT governance principles and decision-making hierarchy;
- an information strategy derived from the business strategy;
- IT risk management in the context of the organisation's overall risk management framework;
- software applications: how business applications are developed, authorised, acquired and managed;
- ICT architecture (integration and standardisation) to meet the requirements of the information and applications strategy.
- ICT infrastructure/technology: how IT services are specified developed, authorised, acquired and managed – what services should be outsourced, why and to whom?
- ICT investment and project governance: given the IT strategy, which IT initiatives (including outsourcing initiatives) should be implemented and how should they be managed?
- information compliance and security: the criteria for securing information and achieving legal/regulatory compliance.

Calder suggests the establishment of four governance committees for managing IT and IT projects. Three committees of importance to an outsourcing project are:

- the board steering committee;

---

[23] *IT Governance: Guidelines for Directors*, Calder A, IT Governance Ltd, 2005.

13: IT Governance

- the executive committee; and
- the technology committee.

Board steering committee

This comprises a majority of directors and key executives: the chief executive officer, the chief finance officer, the chief information officer and the chief compliance officer.

Broadly, Calder proposes that this committee oversees the entirety of the organisation's IT operations, but singles out area seven – project governance (for instance, an outsourcing project) – as a particularly important area for board oversight and monitoring.

Executive committee

The executive committee assumes responsibility for all other areas and exercises powers of delegation to those with appropriate skills and experience.

This committee comprises: the chief information officer and appropriate business managers with the 'single goal: leveraging competitive advantage for the organisation through the cost-effective use of (the most advanced possible) IT – or whatever the board suggests.'[24]

---

[24] *IT Governance: Guidelines for Directors,* Calder A, IT Governance Ltd, 2005.

13: IT Governance

Technology committee

Technical issues are the responsibility of a committee consisting:

> ... primarily of IT staff (although business managers with relevant views and input should be welcomed) necessarily appropriately qualified staff who have adequate theoretical and practical knowledge of each of the key technologies mapped in the enterprise architecture...[25]

The IT Governance Ltd framework[26] identifies six IT governance issues that the board needs to address to ensure value, compliance and risk control. They are:

- Business strategy
- Risk
- IT strategy
- Change
- Information and technology balance sheet
- Operations.

Each issue identifies a number of topics for governance and management and is linked to a number of measures to govern, control, manage and deliver IT services.

The IT Governance Institute

The IT Governance Institute suggests a governance model framework[27] based on IT's delivery of value and mitigation

---

[25] *IT Governance: Guidelines for Directors*, Calder A, IT Governance Ltd, 2005.
[26] *IT Governance Framework: Toolkit v 2.0 (Calder-Moir)*, IT Governance Ltd, available at: www.itgovernance.co.uk.
[27] *Board Briefing on IT Governance, 2nd Edition*, ©2003 IT Governance Institute. All rights reserved. Used by permission

13: IT Governance

of IT risk. It proposes five key areas for IT governance. Appendix E defines them as consisting of five headings:

- Strategic alignment
- Value delivery
- IT resource management
- Risk management
- Performance management.

The governance framework comprises:

- the board of directors;
- an IT strategy committee;
- the CEO;
- business executives;
- the CIO;
- an IT steering committee;
- a technology council; and
- an IT architecture review board.

Each of the roles above, and identified in Appendix E, has defined responsibilities within each of the five functions. For example, within the function of 'strategic alignment', Appendix E expresses the board's responsibilities as: effective strategy planning; alignment of the business and IT strategy; and ensuring organisational structures complement the business model and direction.

13: IT Governance

Capgemini

Capgemini[28] suggests that both organisation and supplier maintain corresponding IT governance frameworks.

- One strategic board: comprising executive sponsors setting the strategic aims of the relationship and overseeing the effectiveness of the contract.
- Managerial board(s): focusing on setting standards, ensuring compliance and maintaining the value of the relationship.
- Operational board(s): addressing implementation functions, such as project management and service delivery.

Such a structure defines roles, responsibility and accountability. As passing time introduces new requirements, the structure is flexible enough to respond effectively.

Typical changes may involve: the need for innovation; extension of the features of the project; and response to the changing needs of the commercial market.

Other frameworks

Various organisations have provided different models of IT governance frameworks, and, of course, as every organisation is different with correspondingly different IT strategies, it would be unlikely that one model would be sufficiently comprehensive to fit all circumstances.

---

[28] *Governing Success: An Integrated Approach to IT Governance and Service Management*, Capgemini, 2008.

13: IT Governance

Some general principles that emerge in respect of IT governance frameworks are that IT governance issues to be addressed include:

- IT and business strategies;
- risk and compliance strategies;
- implementation and performance frameworks;
- monitoring, reporting and auditing processes;
- value delivery;
- resource allocation.

The frameworks most commonly advocated for implementation comprise:

- the board of directors to identify, set and drive the strategy;
- a management board to ensure implementation and compliance;
- a technology board to bring expertise where required for the success of the project;
- an operational board to address implementation;
- a project team to progress and manage the project; and
- a programme management team to manage the portfolio of IT projects currently undertaken by the organisation.

How do such frameworks apply to outsourcing the IT function? These frameworks, although they may be different in construction, each have the same objective: management of the IT function and application of IT governance principles. Outsourcing an IT function falls squarely within this category. By outsourcing IT, the organisation does not relinquish ownership of the function; it delegates the function to a third party for payment of a fee. It is a project in exactly the same way as any project undertaken by an in-house IT department.

13: IT Governance

As one of the key factors causing outsourcing projects to fail lies in the failure to observe governance principles, the implementation of a governance framework must be a priority. However, any governance framework is unlikely to be successful without appropriate tools – standards and methodologies – to support its implementation.

Governance framework tools

Unless IT governance frameworks are organised, managed and implemented to a consistent standard and in accordance with mutually accepted corporate governance principles, there is a danger that the cohesion of the outsourcing relationship will be put at risk as commercial pressures and conflicting interests emerge.

Certain standards and methodologies have been developed to address the need for a systematic application of IT governance principles.

In the context of an outsourcing project, they establish principles by which an organisation develops, implements, manages, controls, monitors, audits and reviews the project during its lifetime.

CobiT

CobiT (Control Objectives for Information and related Technology) is a standard for best practice and is essentially an IT governance control framework to maximise investment in IT and provide controls for the avoidance of error.

Its objective is '...to research, develop, publicise and promote an authoritative, up-to-date, internationally

13: IT Governance

accepted IT governance control framework for adoption by enterprises....'[29]

The basic principle is founded on the requirements of the business which drive the investment in IT resources and that are used by IT processes to deliver enterprise information. Its premise is that the CobiT framework helps to ensure alignment with business requirements.

ISO/IEC 38500:2008

Each of the governance frameworks described above may be complemented by certification under ISO/IEC 38500:2008, the international standard for Corporate Governance of Information Technology.

The British Standards Institution's website[30] describes the standard as providing:

> ... guiding principles for directors of organisations (including owners, board members, directors, partners, senior executives, or similar) on the effective, efficient and acceptable use of information technology within their organisations. This standard applies to the governance of management principles (and decisions) relating to the information and communications services used by an organisation. These processes could be controlled by IT specialists within the organisation or external service providers, or by business units within the organisation.

It is clear from the last sentence of this introduction that the standard is wide enough in its scope to apply to suppliers of outsourced IT functions.

---

[29] *CobiT 4.1 Framework*, IT Governance Institute, May 2007.
[30] Permission to reproduce from ISO/IEC 38500:2008 is granted by BSI (see p. 271).

13: IT Governance

The purpose of the standard is expressed as:

- Assuring stakeholders (including customers, shareholders and employees) that if the standard is followed, they can have confidence in the organisation's corporate governance of IT;
- Informing and guiding directors in providing the use of IT in their organisation;
- Providing a basis for objective evaluation of the corporate governance of IT.

The benefit of achieving certification is expressed to be in addressing the management of risk more effectively. By applying the standard's principles, the board will be assisted in balancing risks and encouraging opportunities arising from the use of IT; and the risk of directors not fulfilling their obligations is mitigated by giving due attention to the model and properly applying the principles.

The objective of the standard is to provide a framework of principles for directors to use when evaluating, directing and monitoring the use of IT. The standard is a framework to enable those at the highest levels in organisations to fulfil their legal, regulatory and ethical obligations.

Users of the standard are advised to familiarise themselves with the principles of the Cadbury Report and the OECD Principles of Corporate Governance. The standard is designed for use by organisations of all sizes.

The standard enshrines six principles for good corporate governance of IT which express preferred behaviour to guide decision-making. It is not prescriptive, in that it refers only to what should happen, not how it is implemented, as the latter depends on each individual organisation.

The six principles are:

13: IT Governance

- **Responsibility:** the understanding and acceptance within the organisation of responsibilities for both the supply of and demand for, IT.
- **Strategy:** the organisation's business strategy takes into account the capabilities of IT and its strategic plans for IT satisfy the needs of its business strategy.
- **Acquisition:** the organisation's decision-making on IT is based on valid reasoning: appropriate analysis balancing benefits opportunities, risks and cost.
- **Performance:** the organisation's IT is able to support the provision of its services at suitable levels and quality to meet business needs.
- **Conformance:** the organisation's IT complies with mandatory legislation with clearly defined, implemented and enforced policies.
- **Human behaviour:** the organisation's IT policies, practices and procedures recognise the needs of, and show respect for, personnel in the process.

In defining the framework for good governance, the duties of the directors are assigned three tasks:

- evaluation of current and future use of it;
- preparation and implementation of plans to ensure that IT meets business objectives;
- the monitoring of conformance to policies and performance against the plans.

While this standard is dedicated to the development and implementation of an IT governance framework, it does not exclude the adoption of other standards by the organisation or supplier.

Each organisation is different and each IT project is different. For instance, in an outsourcing project, there will

13: IT Governance

doubtless be IT security issues, but this does not mean that the only standard to be applied should relate to IT security. More than one standard may be adopted. The important point is that each standard integrates with, and complements, any other standard which is adopted and that each supplements IT governance principles.

How may the six principles, enshrined in ISO/IEC 38500:2008, be applied to the board's role in an outsourcing project? It is worth restating that the general governance role of any board is to set the strategy, establish and oversee lines of responsibility and accountability, ensure transparent decision-making, pay regard to stakeholder interests and adopt an appropriate risk management strategy.

These principles also apply to the governance of IT projects, with the crucial additional requirement that the project must remain aligned with the business objectives set out in the board's strategy.

In the context of ISO/IEC 38500:2008, the role of the board will vary in its detail according to the model, length and complexity of the outsourcing project. However, below are set out some general applications for each principle.

Responsibility

Determining the need for IT within an organisation in order to compete in the market, provide an effective service to customers and protect stakeholder interests is a key responsibility for the board. The board must decide how the organisation's IT function is to operate in order to meet supply and demand. As part of its strategic deliberations, the board is, therefore, responsible for deciding whether an

13: IT Governance

in-house IT function is adequate, or whether part, or whole, of the function should be outsourced.

The board then needs to decide the outsourcing model: whether through a traditional outsourcing contract; or by adopting a 'utility' approach with the Cloud model; or a combination of the two; and, further, whether a dedicated service or multi-tenanted service is most appropriate.

Strategy

As part of the decision to outsource, the board must determine the organisation's business strategy and assess the extent to which its IT function is capable of achieving business objectives and meeting the needs of the business strategy.

The board must assess the business case for outsourcing. This involves, for example:

- assessment of the organisation's current IT function;
- assessment of how an outsourcing project might better meet business needs and achieve business objectives;
- identification of the appropriate outsourcing model;
- determination of the degree of outsourcing;
- determination of the role of personnel affected by the decision; and
- identification of benefits to end-users and stakeholders.

Acquisition

The board must be able to base any decision regarding the IT function on a clear analysis of the advantages and disadvantages, together with associated risks and costs.

13: IT Governance

The board must, therefore, have a clear rationale for selecting an outsourcing strategy, based on a sound business case underpinned by the application of corporate and IT governance principles.

In this context, the board should examine four areas:

- the soundness of the business case for outsourcing as a strategy and the development and implementation of a risk management strategy;
- the IT case for outsourcing, having regard to, for example: the competition; the interests of stakeholders and end-users; and the viability of existing IT in meeting business needs;
- the operational implications of outsourcing on the organisation, for example: the effect on personnel; the need to create a qualified retained IT department; and the need to acquire skills to manage supplier relationships;
- the financial implications including, for example: a cost/benefit calculation of outsourcing IT; the cost of compliance with legal, regulatory and industry codes, such as legal expenses; and the need to engage personnel with different skills for managing the retained IT department and supplier relationships.

The conclusions reached by the board under this category will be critical to the establishment of the business case.

Performance

The board must decide how the organisation's IT function is to support and sustain the services it provides to end-users to acceptable levels of both volume and quantity, if it is to compete effectively and protect stakeholder interest.

13: IT Governance

In this context, the board should examine, for example:

- the 'fitness-for-purpose' of the organisation's existing IT function in terms of its ability to maintain and develop service levels and quality;
- the skills and capabilities of the organisation's current personnel in terms of maintaining and developing service levels and quality;
- the most appropriate outsourcing model for maintaining and developing service levels and quality;
- the availability of management and personnel with the skills and experience to address contract and SLA management needs, such as auditing qualifications, whether in the traditional or Cloud outsourcing models;
- the need to transfer personnel for performance of the outsourcing project, or to import personnel for management of the project;
- the availability of assets, such as software, to maintain and develop service levels and quality;
- the ability of potential suppliers, their management and operational competence, their skills and experience in maintaining and developing the service levels and quality required by the organisation; and
- the resources available to potential suppliers for maintaining and developing service levels and quality, including certification under relevant standards.

Conformance

The board must assess the implications and need for legal and regulatory compliance in respect of its IT function.

In the context of an outsourcing project, this has particularly onerous implications – but compliance is a

13: IT Governance

critical governance principle which should be applied with special rigour in respect of outsourcing projects.

In this context, the board should examine, for example:

- the implications of any compliance required with the DPA;
- the implications of any compliance required with TUPE 2006;
- the implications of any compliance required with the CDPA;
- the implications of any compliance required with industry, trade or professional codes and standards.

It is the board's responsibility to establish the full extent of the organisation's potential exposure to liability for non-compliance. Not only does non-compliance expose an organisation to civil and criminal proceedings, in certain circumstances, the reputation of the organisation may be catastrophically damaged.

The board should, therefore, promulgate policies within its own organisation governing, for instance, the management of data securely and confidentially, and copyright and software licences.

Of equal importance is the need for the directors to ensure that any prospective supplier is fully aware of the requirements of relevant legal and regulatory requirements and can provide evidence of compliance. In all outsourcing projects, this is critical, but never more so than in an outsourcing model based on the Cloud model, where, in particular, data is stored in farms of virtualised servers and there is a real risk of data mismanagement.

13: IT Governance

Human behaviour

It is widely recognised in the context of information security management that the great majority of incidents arise from human error. It is, therefore, the responsibility of the board to ensure that personnel are trained to understand their responsibilities and obligations in the organisation.

This is a key principle of corporate governance and it begins with the board's responsibility to establish, throughout the organisation, clearly defined lines of responsibility and accountability.

Where specific areas of guidance are needed, the board should promulgate suitable policies and procedures to be observed. In an outsourcing project, this approach should be considered specifically in the following circumstances:

- for personnel recruited or deployed in a newly-formed retained IT department;
- for personnel recruited or deployed in a newly-formed department for the management of the contract and SLA;
- for personnel recruited or deployed in a newly-formed department for the management of the organisation's relationship with the supplier; and
- for personnel who are redeployed to the supplier's premises under the terms of the outsourcing contract and who will need training and guidance on any new areas of responsibilities.

Summary

This analysis of the six principles of ISO/IEC 38500:2008 illustrates that the board has a critical role to perform in the implementation and management of an outsourcing project.

13: IT Governance

In each of the six areas, the board is required to initiate, lead and develop the strategy and operational performance of the organisation. This applies both to an in-house IT department and the outsourcing of IT in a traditional or Cloud model.

In an outsourcing project, the function of the board as creator, leader and driver of the project's strategy is vital to the success of the project. It is essential that the board retains tight control as the project develops because, by the very nature of an outsourcing contract, an important element of the organisation's function is being entrusted to the supplier.

COSO – Committee of Sponsoring Organisations of the Treadway Commission

The Treadway Commission was created in 1985 under sponsorship from a number of influential finance auditing and accounting organisations. Its objectives were to identify key causes of fraudulent financial reporting and make recommendations for its prevention.

The committee of sponsoring organisations (COSO) (*www.coso.org*) provided a framework of criteria for identifying the need for internal controls and the evaluation of their effectiveness. The subsequent report, *Internal Control - Integrated Framework* was published in 1992 and is known as the COSO framework.

What is meant by internal control? COSO defines this as:

... a process effected by an entity's board of directors, management and other personnel. This process is designed to provide reasonable assurance regarding the achievement of objectives in effectiveness and efficiency of operations, reliability

13: IT Governance

of financial reporting and compliance with applicable law and regulations.[31]

This definition is followed by four observations:

- Internal control is a process. It is a means to an end, not an end in itself.
- Internal control is not merely documented by policy manuals and forms.
- Internal control can provide only reasonable assurance, not absolute assurance, to an entity's management and board.
- Internal control is geared to the achievements of objectives in one or more separate but overlapping categories.

COSO has been linked with the provisions section 404 of the Sarbanes-Oxley Act 2002 requiring management to reveal any financial weakness that prevents assurance and that an organisation's internal financial control is adequate where one or more vulnerabilities have been disclosed.

The framework underpinning the management's decision-making process must be recognised as having been devised by a body that has tested the procedures and obtained public recognition.

It is important to understand that certification of standards and the implementation of methodologies are not IT governance, although they may be evidence of this. IT governance is the framework of leadership, organisational infrastructure and business processes. Standards and methodologies are tools employed in implementing an IT governance framework.

---

[31] *www.coso.org/resources.htm*

13: IT Governance

IT governance and service management

It is important to understand how the management of the outsourcing service is linked to IT governance.

In an IT outsourcing project, there are two elements of service management: the provision of the service by the supplier; and the management of the service provision by the organisation's retained IT function.

The retained IT department has knowledge of the organisation and is accountable for implementing policy as required by the board and senior management.

The supplier has knowledge and experience of the IT services required by the organisation and is responsible for provision of the outsourced service.

Effective IT service management calls for a best practice infrastructure. ITIL® is well recognised for providing comprehensive documentation on best practice for IT service management (www.itil-officialsite.com). Version 3 of ITIL offers the concept of lifecycle management which takes the user from the design stage to identification of measurable service levels, operation, monitoring, support, data gathering and feedback into the system, moving finally to renewing the cycle with a process of continuous improvement.

The retained IT function may be confronted with many complexities under an outsourcing contract and SLA for which it has neither the skills nor the qualifications. If it is not equipped to fulfil its function, it may be necessary to outsource the function to a suitably qualified supplier.

Implementing IT service management in an IT governance framework enables the accountability of the retained IT

13: IT Governance

function and the responsibility of the supplier to be managed, so that the IT services provided achieve the parties' respective objectives within the project.

The concept of, and need for, an IT governance framework should be recognised by both parties at the outset of an outsourcing project. A governance framework ensures a consistent approach to implementation of the board's strategy. The performance of the retained IT function can be monitored and sufficient skills and resources made available (whether in house or outsourced) to enable the IT function to manage the IT services. At the same time, the supplier's performance can also be monitored and audited.

In this way, a governance framework enables both organisation and supplier to understand each other's objectives and work together for their achievement.

Capgemini[32] is currently involved in some excellent research into issues concerning service integration in outsourcing projects, looking particularly at the IT governance and service management structures that should be implemented between organisation and supplier.

Service standards

Accredit UK[33] has been developed by The National Computing Centre with the help of the British Standards Institution and a wide range of other bodies. It is a standard of excellence for suppliers and purchasers of ICT solutions.

---

[32] *Service Integration - Service Management as a Service*, Capgemini, 29 May 2009.
[33] www.accredituk.com.

13: IT Governance

The standard assesses a business across five stages:

- Business management
- Business direction
- Business generation
- Delivery and operations
- Customer relations.

Standards are written for large and small purchasers and suppliers of ICT services. Businesses must prove general business competence and technical expertise.

The standard covers the following segments:

- ICT consultancy
- Software product design and development
- Solutions design and development
- Communications (network design and installation)
- ICT goods manufacturing and repair
- Wholesale trade and distribution
- New media and e-commerce
- Information assurance
- Information and broadcast services.

The standard is defined at two levels:

- general expectations: specifying general areas of good practice across all segments; and
- segment-specific expectations: specifying conformance requirements in individual segments.

Accredit UK is the sign of trust for the IT industry, delivered by the National Computing Centre. It is a quality standard that shows purchasers of IT that they can trust any supplier who holds the standard to deliver first-class solutions.

13: IT Governance

Conclusion

The establishment of an IT governance framework does not mean that a project can then be left to run itself without supervision or monitoring of progress and execution of the agreed strategy.

At all levels of the governance framework, strategic, managerial and operational, there should be corresponding levels of responsibility and accountability, so that the parties to the contract can perform their respective obligations in a spirit of mutual understanding and co-operation.

Calder[34] suggests this should be:

… a specific responsibility, given time on the agenda with adequate internal and external audit reporting to committee members who have sufficient understanding of the issues to question findings and to give directions about appropriate steps and actions.

The principles of corporate governance, if observed, ensure that organisations are complying with requirements of transparency, accountability and stakeholder interest in respect of business activities.

Corporate governance principles are extended by the concept of IT governance and various tools, comprising standards and methodologies. IT governance principles are intended to cement a mutually beneficial relationship in which the mutual interests and benefits provided by an outsourcing project enable the parties' respective expectations to be realised.

---

[34] *IT Governance: Guidance for Directors*, Calder A, IT Governance Ltd, 2005.

13: IT Governance

The IT governance models considered in this chapter offer some suggestions on how to construct an IT governance framework consistently.

Remembering that the key issues for corporate governance are:

- transparency;
- responsibility;
- accountability;
- risk management including compliance; and
- shareholder value;

an IT governance framework begins with a board committee formed of members qualified to direct key stages of the outsourcing project. Beneath the board committee may be a number of other committees which address specific aspects of the process. These have been variously identified as:

- a strategy committee to direct overall strategy of the project and ensure it remains aligned to the organisation's objectives;
- a steering committee to navigate and manage the organisation through the various stages of the project;
- an IT committee to ensure that the IT services to be provided by the supplier meet the objectives of the organisation's strategy and address the needs of the retained IT department; and
- a standards committee to identify relevant standards and methodologies for adoption for the purposes of the project.

Many organisations invest vast sums over long periods of time in IT outsourcing projects. It is important that the need

13: IT Governance

to extend governance frameworks to include an outsourcing project also includes suppliers within the framework.

A key requirement that emerges from the introduction of an IT governance framework is that whatever framework is adopted, it should, as far as is possible, be mirrored by both organisation and supplier. In this way, a consistent approach can be achieved over the various stages of the outsourcing project.

Corporate governance establishes a framework for the management and organisation at board level. IT governance principles establish a framework for the implementation of IT strategies determined by the board.

Like any other project, outsourcing is a project to which governance principles should be applied. The next chapter addresses project governance.

CHAPTER 14: PROJECT GOVERNANCE

The outsourcing of an IT function is a project. In order to understand the meaning and implications of project governance, it is important to understand the meaning of a project.

Definition

It is difficult to find a comprehensive, universally accepted definition of the word 'project'. In essence, a project is an undertaking designed to be performed within specific time limits and with specific objectives, most frequently by a team of individuals with specialist skills that enable the achievement of the project's objectives.

Objective

These characteristics are all recognisable in an IT outsourcing project. The clear objective of such a project is invariably to select a supplier who will improve or complement the organisation's deployment of IT for its business purposes.

Time frame

An outsourcing project must be managed within an agreed time frame. Having made the decision to outsource, the planning process identifies the stages by which the project must be completed within an IT governance framework.

14: Project Governance

Teams

An outsourcing project has a number of different aspects to be managed: oversight, planning and implementation. In terms of an IT outsourcing project, one or more teams may be needed for these functions, and at a more detailed level, specialist teams may be needed for managing the outsourcing contract, the SLA and other specialist aspects.

Change

The impact of an implemented IT outsourcing project will inevitably involve change for the organisation. This may occur in a number of ways:

- redeployment of existing personnel;
- recruitment of new personnel, such as contract managers, to manage the outsourcing project;
- closure or re-organisation of the IT department; or
- creation of a retained IT department.

Every organisation has different requirements of an IT outsourcing project and the consequential changes for every organisation will be different.

Project management includes the management of change through a combination of management and planning.

There are numerous causes for projects failing. Some originate from characteristics particular to the parties to the transaction but the majority are generic. The Office of Government Commerce[35] identifies some strategic issues:

---

[35] *Common Causes of Project Failure*, Office of Government Commerce, 2006.

14: Project Governance

- lack of clear links between the project and the organisation's key strategic priorities;
- lack of clear senior management, ownership and leadership;
- lack of effective engagement with stakeholders;
- lack of skills and proven approach to project and risk management;
- inadequate attention to breaking development and implementation into manageable steps;
- evaluation of proposals driven by initial price rather than long-term value;
- lack of understanding of, and contact with, the supply industry at senior levels;
- lack of effective project team integration between clients, the supplier team and the supply chain.

Other causes, at operational level, include: wastage of resources; escalation of cost; incorrect priorities; insufficient resources; failure to take account of change in scope; inadequate delegation; overlooking key objectives; excessive focus on detail; and inadequately qualified personnel.

Governance

Like corporate governance and IT governance, project governance is a framework for the delivery and achievement of a project's objectives through application of the governance principles of transparency, responsibility, accountability, compliance and risk management.

Implementation involves securing and managing the required resources, adapting to change, and monitoring and auditing performance. In the governance hierarchy, project governance sits below corporate governance, alongside IT governance, and above project management.

All parts of the organisation involved in a project should be integrated with the project governance framework. It is a cross-organisational process where appropriate input from the required quarters helps to ensure the success of the project.

Objectives

These causes of failure provide a clear indication of the objectives that a project governance framework should achieve.

- First, the project must remain aligned with the strategic objectives of the business for its duration.
- Second, throughout the project, there must be a continuous auditing and monitoring of resources against cost.
- Third, resources must be deployed, so that the project provides maximum value and benefit for the organisation.
- Fourth, the organisation must take a formal and structured approach to risk assessment and risk management.
- Fifth, the organisation should apply recognised best practice project management methodologies.

Project governance features

What are the key features of a project governance framework? They are based on the same principles as corporate governance and IT governance: responsibility,

14: Project Governance

accountability and transparency and in many respects project governance features will mirror them, although in a different context.

Alan Calder[36] suggests the key features required to establish a project governance framework are:

- executive leadership;
- board committee for approval monitoring and audit;
- clear outcome/requirements specification and ongoing collaboration between informed customers/users and project staff;
- clear project proposal, approval and personalisation processes that are strong on identification of business purpose, tie in to the enterprise IT architecture and objective return on investment and performance criteria;
- clear allocation of responsibilities – including an experienced project manager – and accountabilities (contractual where necessary, with adequate penalties);
- tested project management methodology and experienced practitioners;
- objective resource allocation planning and (budget) commitment;
- objectively measurable (and verifiable) milestones;
- independent monitoring and board reporting;
- staggered release of funds in line with milestone delivery;
- communications strategy with detailed, well thought-out plans;

---

[36] *IT Governance Today: A Practitioner's Guide*, Calder A, IT Governance Ltd, 2005.

- a risk management plan that includes fallback procedures for non-achievement of key milestones as well as dealing with business continuity, information security and regulatory compliance issues.

Projects are governed by time and resource constraints which can often be the cause of failure. Projects, therefore, need certain features that will provide the prospect of success. Examples include:

- effective sponsorship;
- clear objectives,
- suitably skilled and competent personnel;
- a widely recognised methodology;
- sound management principles;
- clearly defined lines of responsibility and accountability;
- awareness of stakeholder interest; and
- a careful analysis of the organisation's existing portfolio.

These governance criteria must be applied to each stage of an outsourcing project. They were identified earlier as: the selection of the outsourcing strategy; the selection of the supplier; the tendering, negotiation and due diligence process; the definition of the terms of the contract and SLA; the management of the contract and SLA; the management of change control; and the termination process.

Project governance tools

A project is unlikely to be effective unless the stages are administered or managed in an ordered and methodical manner, and applied with a methodology designed to underpin the governance of projects.

14: Project Governance

Project governance methodology is a method of applying governance principles to the management of a project in order to maximise the chance of the project fulfilling its business objective.

Various project management IT solutions are available. IT solutions do not of themselves provide an IT or project governance framework. They support it. IT solutions are aids to implementing IT and project governance principles, by providing comprehensive management processes to ensure that a project is managed competently and capably. In the context of project management, an IT solution is a tool for managing a project in a particular way or with a particular methodology. An IT solution is not the methodology itself.

PRINCE2®

The most popularly applied methodology in respect of project management has the acronym PRINCE® (Projects in Controlled Environments).

PRINCE® was originally established in 1989 by the Central Computer and Telecommunications Agency, subsequently named the Office of Government Commerce. The second version – PRINCE2® – was published in 1996 and comprised contributions from some 150 European organisations. The website of the PRINCE® foundation is at www.prince2.com.

14: Project Governance

The latest version of PRINCE2® was published in June 2009[37]. It is a processed-based project management standard used widely by the UK government for providing best practice guidance on project management.

It introduces seven key themes, or components, of project management that need continual monitoring and review and that focus on:

- Business case
- Organisation
- Planning
- Project risk
- Progress monitoring
- Quality control
- Issues and changes.

These themes are supported by 'processes' which describe what needs to be done, when and by whom. The processes are:

- Starting up a project
- Directing a project
- Initiating a project
- Controlling a stage
- Managing a stage boundary
- Closing a project.

The standard also addresses and offers guidance on the environment in which the project is being undertaken and includes: projects in a programme; commercial

---

[37] *Managing and Successfully Directing Projects with PRINCE2™*, Murray A, Outperform; © TSO 2009; © PRINCE2 2009; Overview Brochure.

14: Project Governance

customer/supplier relationships; multi-owned projects; alignment with other lifecycle models and bodies of knowledge; and project scale.

The standard also considers the essential roles in the management of a project: the project board, senior user, executive, senior supplier, project manager, team manager, project assurance and project support.

The standard is supported by process-based checklists aligned to the governance principles adopted by the Association of Project Managers.

Finally, guidance is offered to senior managers who sponsor projects, including suggestions as to what makes a good project board, suggested agendas for project board reviews, a checklist of key decisions for each project board review and pre and post-project responsibilities.

The standard is supported by two guides:

- *Managing Successful Projects with PRINCE2®* for those who work on projects on a daily basis;
- *Directing Successful Projects with PRINCE2®* for those directing or sponsoring projects.

PRINCE2® can be applied to all types of project and can be tailored for application to small or large and complex projects. Its key focus is on the business case for the project. This includes the interests of the customer (the organisation conducting the project and benefiting from the result) and the user who will operate the final product or service.

PRINCE2® may be more appropriate for more complicated projects. A relatively straightforward outsourcing of a

14: Project Governance

single IT function might not justify the application of each aspect of PRINCE2®.

In that case, the organisation may have the option of selecting elements of the methodology that most appropriately address the management functions that the project involves. Alternatively, the organisation may select a simpler methodology that is more suitable for less complex projects. The important point is the need to introduce some recognised form of methodology that supports project governance principles.

BS 6079:2002

BS 6079:2002[38] is the current standard of certification relating to project management and provides guidance for general managers, project managers, project support staff, educators and trainers on the planning and execution of projects and the application of project management techniques. The principles and procedures outlined are relevant to all sizes of organisation although not all aspects of every project. BS 6079-1:2002 provides guidance on compliance with the standard.

Work has now begun on an international standard – ISO21500 – which will use BS 6079 as a base standard.

Programme portfolio management

Adhering to project governance principles involves managing all projects in such a way that each project

---

[38] Permission to reproduce from BS 6079:2002 is granted by BSI (see p. 271).

14: Project Governance

observes the principles of project governance. This is sometimes referred to as programme management. A series of projects is sometimes referred to as a portfolio and the expression for their management is programme portfolio management (PPM).

Effective PPM offers flexibility in terms of an organisation's response to market forces. A wider range of solutions becomes available and pricing and investment strategies can be more appropriately assessed. Portfolio management enables an organisation to weigh up the competing issues of risk, cost, investment and resources and to prioritise them accordingly.

PPM organises projects so as to enable an organisation to ensure it adopts the right mix of projects and applies resources appropriate to the needs of each. This results in more tailored control of the strategy and enables the organisation to ensure that the goals of each project remain aligned with corporate obligations.

As the demands made on IT increase, PPM can become a complicated mix of different commitments. It may include: IT services provided by an in-house department with traditional software licences; the use of managed or outsourced services; the employment of dynamic 'on-demand' services or services on demand by subscription, for instance, Cloud computing; or services as part of a multiple supply to a wide range of similar organisations.

Projects run by organisations which do not observe governance principles within a portfolio often reveal certain characteristics, such as inconsistent management; poorly informed personnel; lack of accountability; lack of responsibility; ineffective delegation; duplication of projects; lack of purpose; and widespread ignorance of the objective – or even the existence – of the project

Criteria to be considered for the inclusion of a project within an organisation's portfolio include: the level of business need for the project; the resources available; the size of the project in relation to available resources; any exceptional risks; and the management implications.

Successful PPM:

- helps the correct prioritisation of projects;
- provides responsibility and accountability in the project management process;
- involves co-operation between relevant levels of management, including risk sharing;
- builds trust; and
- encourages teamwork.

PPM is the integrated management of a portfolio of projects designed to deliver strategic business benefit. Its objective is to introduce common criteria for the identification of projects that are justified by a manageable business case. Typical requirements for inclusion might be:

- agreement on the reasons and objectives;
- a project sponsor;
- details of the business benefits;
- risk assessments;
- financial implications;
- resource availability;
- stakeholder interest; and
- the impact of the project both on the organisation's management and any other projects.

14: Project Governance

PPM is organised and conducted by a programme management office (PMO). The PMO provides guidance in respect of, for instance, the suitability of projects for inclusion in the portfolio, the risk profiles of projects, the urgency of projects and the availability of personnel and other resources for commitment to the project.

PPM should be integrated into the organisation's strategic plan because each project is intended to achieve business goals and deliver business benefit. Its function should, therefore, be widely understood at executive and operational level by promulgation from the PMO.

Val IT 2.0

Val IT 2.0 is a governance framework based on CobiT and is concerned with the management of an organisation's portfolio of investments to ensure an adequate return and realisation of value to the organisation.

The framework is a set of management principles and practices that enables an organisation to analyse its business needs and create and manage its portfolio of IT investments to secure maximum financial return and delivery of value to the business.

In essence, the principles of Val IT 2.0 address the need to manage IT investments in a prescribed manner, defining them within categories, tracking their performance, ensuring that stakeholder interests are recognised and assigning lines of accountability during the life of the investment.

An IT outsourcing project is a typical IT investment project that would form part of a portfolio of IT projects to which Val IT could be applied. By adopting a Val IT governance

14: Project Governance

framework for the management of a portfolio which includes an outsourcing project, the organisation can continually monitor, review and evaluate the business value of the project and react appropriately to any adverse developments.

Val IT is explained in a series of white papers published by the IT Governance Institute[39] which set out the various management practices to be adopted in the areas of: value governance, portfolio management and investment management. Ultimately, the board of directors is responsible and accountable to stakeholders in the organisation to ensure that business investments and resources deliver adequate business value.

Project governance technology

The successful management of a project is underpinned by effective standards of performance. IT solutions are available to help assess and manage standards of performance.

A wide variety of project management solutions support PRINCE2®. *Project in a Box* (www.projectinabox.org.uk) provides methodology-led project and programme support solutions to meet the needs of start-ups, single project managers, multi-users and corporate platforms. The software accommodates PRINCE2® processes as standard, as well as other methodologies, but also enables organisations to develop their own processes as stand-alone or in combination with PRINCE2®.

---

[39] www.itgi.org

14: Project Governance

IT Governance Ltd (*www.itgovernance.co.uk*) offers *BugBox*, a workflow issue management tool which is used to control ownership, resolve issues and deliver projects on time. It is scalable for use by a single project manager up to large organisations and can be networked through servers.

Hydra Management (*www.hydra-management.com*) offers *Hydra Manager* as a solution to programme management. The solution enables integrated planning, resource scheduling, dependency analysis, risk management and also supports PRINCE2®.

Project management standards

The Project Management Institute (PMI)[40] has published four standards for project and portfolio management:

- *A Guide to the Project Management Body of Knowledge* (fourth edition): is a set of processes which are claimed to be recognised as generally accepted as good practice.
- *The Organisational Project Management Maturity Model Knowledge Foundation* (second edition): is intended as a set of tools for organisations to measure their maturity against a comprehensive set of best practices.
- *The Standard for Program Management* (second edition) develops knowledge areas for particular programs and includes governance and audit issues.
- *The Standard for Portfolio Management* (second edition) addresses issues of governance and risk.

---

[40] *www.pmi.org*

14: Project Governance

The Project Management Body of Knowledge Guide (PMBOK Guide) extends to almost a dozen standards, some of which have just been updated.

Conclusion

The previous chapter identified IT governance frameworks that might underpin an IT outsourcing project, and identified a number of committees and teams that might be appropriate in the development process.

To this framework should be added the project team. Its composition will depend upon the nature of the project, but is likely to include:

- a senior project manager
- a contract manager
- an SLA manager
- a compliance manager
- a finance manager; and
- a relationship manager.

An IT outsourcing project may form one component in a range of an organisation's portfolio of projects. For consistency, governance principles should be applied to the management of a portfolio of projects: transparency, responsibility and accountability, alignment with business goals and allocation of resources so as to achieve the objectives of each project.

PRINCE2® is the most widely recognised of a number of project governance methodologies and is probably the most appropriate for an outsourcing project. Each organisation must decide on a methodology most appropriate for the

14: Project Governance

projects in its portfolio. Projects differ in nature, complexity and importance for an organisation.

Project governance technology supports the effective management of projects and, therefore, can assist organisations in the application of governance principles. In applying IT governance principles, the board, and the various committees and teams accountable to it, should adopt IT solutions that support programme management, project management and performance management.

An outsourcing contract itself may be complex. It may also be one of a number of IT projects within a programme portfolio. It may also form part of a range of differing types of outsourcing model, for example, single tenant, multi-tenant, traditional or Cloud computing model. Whatever the model of outsourcing contract, governance principles should be applied at project, IT and corporate governance levels.

It is also highly desirable that, if at all possible, the supplier provides evidence of the application of similar governance principles, supported by appropriate methodologies and governance technology; an appropriate area to address at the tendering and due diligence stage of the pre-contract process.

CHAPTER 15: RISK ASSESSMENT

A fundamental component of effective corporate governance is the assessment and management of risk. The key issues for organisations to address when considering an outsourcing strategy were considered in Chapter 3 (the business considerations) and Chapter 4 (the outsourcing decision).

These issues were collectively grouped in categories of: strategy, technology, compliance, operations and finance. Later, the key risks to be considered when implementing an outsourcing strategy will be analysed in the same categories.

However, in order to manage risk issues arising from an outsourcing strategy, it is important, first, to understand the main principles of risk assessment.

Project failure

The most potentially damaging risk arising in IT outsourcing projects is that of project failure. Projects that ultimately fail after continuing for many years and involving many millions of pounds, not to mention the human endeavour, are damaging to both organisation and supplier alike. It is, therefore, important that any organisation embarking on such a project has a full understanding of the key issues that give rise to the potential for project failure.

15: Risk Assessment

Common causes that emerge from a variety of surveys and practical experience suggest that the most frequent causes of outsourcing project failure are:

- failure to analyse the supplier's ability to perform to the required standards;
- misunderstanding the importance of managing the supplier relationship;
- failure to factor in the cost of the retained IT department; and
- inadequate due diligence procedures.

Many outsourcing projects are approached with differing and conflicting objectives: the organisation wants reduced costs; the supplier wants higher profit; the organisation wants access to greater skills; the supplier wants cheaper personnel, so that profit margins are maintained.

Not all risks lead to project failure. Many risks may surround an organisation's expectations, or the value of the project, or the benefit of the project, or the profitability of the project – and are not necessarily fatal to the overall success of the project.

Factors leading to the ultimate failure and termination of an outsourcing project can be identified as: strategy, planning, implementation, management and governance.

Strategy

Typical issues arising within this category include: incorrect business motives for outsourcing; unrealistic expectations; misalignment of the outsourcing project with business goals; inadequate involvement of shareholders,

15: Risk Assessment

stakeholders, employees and end-users; and a mismatch of the parties' respective cultures.

Planning

Typical issues include: too much or too little attention to detail in the planning process; poor quality decision making at the planning stage; inadequate valuation of cost in relation to benefits; and ineffectively conducted due diligence.

Implementation

Typical issues include: failure to adhere to the defined scope of the project; failure to approach implementation on a systematic and methodical basis in progressive stages; over-enthusiastic approaches to the project in the early stages which are not maintained; and lack of personnel with adequate skills and qualifications.

Management

Typical issues include: inadequate monitoring, review and audit procedures in respect of contract and SLA performance; failure to maintain adequate levels of communication with both personnel and supplier; and failure of the organisation to manage multiple suppliers.

Governance

Typical issues include failure by the board to: supervise the project with due transparency and accountability towards shareholders, stakeholders, employees and end-users;

15: Risk Assessment

define and enforce areas of responsibility and accountability in the management of the project; ensure implementation, monitoring, reviewing and auditing procedures from the top downwards and from the bottom upwards; adopt and execute a suitably comprehensive risk assessment and management strategy.

A common theme runs through these five components. Each of the examples under each heading involves, to a greater or lesser extent, a failure of management in some way and each could be avoided with the establishment of an appropriate governance infrastructure equipped with suitably trained and qualified personnel.

Ultimately, good governance is the method by which an outsourcing project will proceed successfully. A significant component of good governance is effective risk assessment and management.

Risk assessment

The importance of risk management was recognised in the Turnbull Report produced by the Institute of Chartered Accountants, and revisions to which were published in October 2005[41].

The fundamental thinking behind the Turnbull Report is that risk management should be a consciously planned strategy by the directors. The strategy should include a system of checks, balances and internal controls to protect

---

[41] *Internal Control: Revised Guidance for Directors on the Combined Code*, Financial Reporting Council, October 2005, available at: *www.frc.org.uk/documents/pagemanager/frc/Revised%20Turnbull%20 Guidance%20October%202005.pdf*.

15: Risk Assessment

the financial interests of the organisation. Further, these checks and balances should be regularly reviewed across all areas of the organisation's operations, for instance, strategic, technological, financial, or compliance.

In broad terms, in the context of outsourcing, risk can be regarded as any issue that might jeopardise an organisation's achievement of its business objectives.

Risk concepts

There are two types of risk. Strategic risk involves the overall direction of the organisation and its position in the marketplace. Operational risk involves the proper functioning and 'operation' of the organisation.

In some situations, a risk may be both strategic and operational. For instance, the risk of non-compliance with the DPA may be a strategic risk in that a prosecution may have implications for the reputation of the organisation. At the same time, it is also an operational risk because it involves the training and education of personnel in the relevant compliance procedures.

There are different forms of risk. Pure risks are those which simply incur losses. Speculative risk may bring losses or gains. An organisation may take speculative risks as part of its business strategy. Some risks have foreseeable consequences and are generally easier to manage. The consequences of other risks are less clear.

Risk can also arise unexpectedly having not appeared previously as an identifiable threat. This is especially so in the commercial environment where organisations are dependent on circumstances outside their control. Risk might arise from a sudden and quite unforeseeable change

15: Risk Assessment

in the market for which no adequate provision appears in an outsourcing contract or SLA.

Risk affects all organisations. Small organisations are more likely to be affected by risks that threaten their survival. Risks in larger organisations may arise simply from their size and complexity. In assessing where risk lies, an organisation should ask three questions:

- What is the worst that could happen?
- How likely is it to happen?
- Are procedures in place to prevent its occurrence?

Risk may affect an organisation adversely in two ways: impacting on the day to day performance and the profitability of its function, and on business continuity. In an IT outsourcing project, an inadequately managed SLA may seriously affect the organisation's service to end-users. Failure to undertake sufficient due diligence that might reveal the likely financial collapse of the supplier could affect the ability of the organisation to continue in business.

Assessing risk

The first step in assessing risk is to identify where risks arise in the implementation of a strategy. For example, in the case of outsourcing, the organisation will want to satisfy itself that a supplier is not providing similar services to a competitor, or that no compliance issues arise in the use of any software by the supplier.

Once a risk is identified, a decision must be made on its level and the resources required for its management. The risk must be analysed by recognising the threat, assessing

15: Risk Assessment

the consequences for the organisation should it materialise and identifying the organisation's level of exposure.

For example, in the case of an SLA where the supplier's performance levels may be inadequate, the exposure is to immediate and future loss of profitability. The vulnerability is the absence of any performance management strategy with which to monitor the supplier's performance.

A risk assessment can be undertaken in a number of ways. A mathematical formula may be applied to identify the likelihood of risk arising. In its simplest form, a score of 1-10 is applied to a particular risk.

A second approach is to conduct an analysis based on decisions in particular circumstances. For example, in an IT outsourcing project, a decision-based assessment may be required regarding the risk to the organisation losing control of its IT competence and becoming overly dependent on the supplier. The decision might be taken to retain the services of in-house expertise, or external consultants, to ensure that the organisation possesses sufficient technological knowledge to be able to manage the supplier.

A third approach involves taking a calculated risk. For example, the organisation might identify the risk of a supplier also supplying services to a competitor. The organisation may take a calculated risk that, despite this, such is the reputation of the supplier's excellent service in the marketplace, the risk is worth taking.

A final element of risk assessment is the human element – a feature that frequently fails to receive adequate consideration. Many operational risks arise from the

15: Risk Assessment

conduct of personnel. It is important to adopt the right approach to personnel management.

Management that is weak and indecisive, or lacks business skills or technical expertise, is unlikely to gain commitment from subordinates in the management of risk issues. A management team which has little experience of technology can hardly be expected to be at the forefront of organising a project which involves the outsourcing of IT. Similarly, a poorly performing management team is unlikely to gain the competitive advantage that properly conducted risk assessment and management can offer.

Assessment objectives

The purpose of risk assessment is to balance the potential benefits of a course of action against the potential risks of a course of action. Accurate risk assessment prevents risks from becoming problems that then develop into crises.

A risk assessment helps to determine how a risk might be managed. There are three options:

- accepting but minimising the impact of a risk;
- transferring responsibility to a third party, for instance, an insurer; or
- eliminating the risk entirely.

The benefits of an accurate risk assessment are significant and affect every area of an organisation's function. They include:

- a better understanding of new and existing risks;
- better business continuity plans;
- higher risk awareness in managing projects;
- potential for identifying opportunities;

15: Risk Assessment

- improved integration of the functions of project management;
- greater team awareness of risk;
- the ability to concentrate on specific issues;
- the capture of enterprise knowledge and know-how;
- recognition of the impact of environmental influences.

Having identified a risk, the next step is to conduct an assessment of its impact.

The risk assessment

A key ingredient of successful risk assessment is the collection of sufficient data on which to base an informed decision. The most obvious source of information will be those most concerned with the function giving rise to the risk. Methods of collating data should include:

- discussion with key personnel concerned with the control of the particular risk;
- circulation of questionnaires to obtain a range of views on particular risks; and
- workshops and focus groups.

It is also important that the correct personnel are approached. In the case of strategic risks, consultation should begin at board level, with input from senior management level. Strategic IT issues should be considered by an IT director. Risks that essentially concern operational IT issues might be considered by an IT manager. When performing a consultation, a full, as opposed to a subjective, perspective of risk should be obtained from as many sources as practical.

15: Risk Assessment

Findings from consultations should be recorded and can then form the basis for a risk control plan. This identifies the relevant person responsible for management of particular risks and the types of solution that might be adopted for their control.

A risk control plan lists the key risks, then profiles and rates them according to severity and priority. It also identifies the measures that the organisation proposes to take to control the risk. The overall objective is to confirm the organisation in the position it occupies before any consequences of the risk are realised.

Typical issues to be considered in devising a plan include:

- the source of the risk;
- the severity of the risk;
- the risk controls to be applied;
- the person(s) or team responsible;
- the action taken; and
- relevant time frames.

This can be documented in a simple spreadsheet, although project management solutions frequently provide applications that enable such data to be recorded, and some risk management solutions provide similar functions.

A risk control plan should be made available to all relevant personnel. Although detailed knowledge may not be necessary, a general awareness of its content and the circumstances in which it is to be invoked within the organisation is advisable.

The systematic application of a set of risk assessment principles enables an organisation to decide how, when and

15: Risk Assessment

where risk management strategies should be developed and implemented.

Having collated and categorised the key risks relating to the development and implementation of an IT outsourcing project, the next stage is to develop and implement a risk management strategy.

The next chapter identifies the principal risks that the organisation will need to address.

CHAPTER 16: IDENTIFYING THE RISKS

Numerous statistics are presented to show that outsourcing risks are either not appreciated or are otherwise mismanaged. One risk issue that is significantly underestimated is the adverse effect that the impact of time can have on an outsourcing project. Some statistics have suggested that as many as 25% of projects fail within two years and as many as 50% in five years.

Typical risks include misalignment of business goals with outsourcing projects, lack of clarity over the scope of the project and inadequate skills and training procedures.

Many executives give too little thought to the risks that may impact on the project and make dangerous assumptions that the due diligence process irons out all the risks ahead of the project, and fail to adopt a sufficiently rigorous approach to risk management.

The extent of outsourcing risk ranges across a wide spectrum of every description: international, legal and compliance, human resources, operations and culture. Whatever the nature of the risk, a common factor in all outsourcing failure can be found − a failure in the management and governance function.

This chapter identifies key risks in the process of outsourcing the IT function. On the basis that every project has different considerations, so every project carries individual risks. The analysis identifies the most common generic risks.

16: Identifying the Risks

The analysis divides risks into the categories of strategic and managerial risk, technology risk, legal and compliance risk, operational risk and financial risk.

Each category is subdivided into two further categories: those risks originating primarily from the organisation and those risks originating primarily from the supplier.

Strategic and managerial risk

This category of risk arises from the failure at board and managerial levels to take account of key factors in identifying a suitable strategy and failure to implement an appropriate management strategy.

Organisation

- Erosion and loss of the organisation's core competence in IT in terms of loss of IT skills, surrendering control to the supplier and becoming locked into dependency on the supplier.
- Failure to align the objective of the project with the goals of the business, resulting in a reduced ability to compete through, for instance, the outsourced functions failing to provide competitive advantage or outsourcing for the wrong market.
- Failure to define business goals and objectives adequately with the result that the purpose of the outsourcing project is misunderstood.
- An outsourcing project based on an inadequate business case, for instance, through an assessment based on inadequate information and data, or insufficient due diligence.

16: Identifying the Risks

- An inadequate assessment of the impact that the implementation of an outsourcing project will have on other aspects of the organisation.
- An inadequately implemented strategic risk and risk management process at board, senior management and operational levels.

Supplier

- A dominant supplier, whether through size, reputation or competence, assuming a dominant position between the parties.
- An inadequately conducted selection and tendering process based on subjective, not business, considerations.
- The selection of a supplier closely linked with the organisation's competitors, or even supplying related to services to competitors.
- The selection of a supplier with a dominant, if not monopolistic, position in the outsourcing marketplace.
- The inability, for whatever reason, of the supplier to understand key aspects of the organisation's complexity.
- Cultural differences between the supplier and the organisation that cannot be reconciled and which adversely affect the successful implementation and operation of the project.
- A dominant position of the supplier, and an over dependency by the organisation within the exit and termination process.

16: Identifying the Risks

Technology risks

These risks arise from the effects of outsourcing the technology and concern its potential impact upon the relationship between the parties and stakeholders.

Organisation

- The loss by the organisation to the supplier of its key IT skills and related intellectual assets leaving the organisation at a significant disadvantage on termination of the project.
- Inadequate specification of IT requirements for the project by the organisation.
- Insufficient information provided by the organisation to enable the supplier to understand the organisation's needs.
- Failure by the organisation to monitor, audit and review the supplier's information security measures.
- Inadequate research of the supplier's service capacity and its ability to meet the organisation's requirements.

Supplier

- Inability of the supplier to implement technological innovations to meet the changing needs of the organisation's end-users.
- The supplier's use of obsolescent or legacy technology to the detriment of its standards of service to the organisation.
- Inadequate standard of IT in place at the time of contracting to ensure that, on implementation of the contract, the supplier is able to comply with the SLA.

16: Identifying the Risks

- Failure by the supplier to understand the organisation's IT requirements.
- Failure by the supplier to implement information security technology measures, processes and procedures to required standards.

Compliance risks

These risks arise from a failure to understand statutory and regulatory provisions that govern certain aspects of the process of outsourcing the IT function. Although not necessarily mandatory, an organisation should view compliance as including industry codes and standards in assessing the risks to which it might be exposed in an outsourcing project.

Organisation

- Failure to ensure that the contract and related documentation specifies the statutory and regulatory provisions (together with relevant industry codes and standards required) with which the supplier is required to comply.
- Failure of the contract to define areas of responsibility between the parties in respect of compliance provisions.

Supplier

- Failure to observe compliance provisions in respect of data handling.
- Failure to provide for and implement a business continuity and disaster recovery strategy.

16: Identifying the Risks

- Failure to comply with the provisions of TUPE 2006.
- Failure to observe provisions regarding copyright and licensing infringements.

Operational risks

Operational risks are those which arise from the 'mechanical' aspects of the development, implementation and termination of the outsourcing project. They are many and various. As every project is different, so will be the corresponding risks. Those identified below are the more typical operational risks associated with an IT outsourcing project.

Organisation

- Inadequate resources in terms of time, skills, personnel and finance allocated to selection and tendering procedures.
- Inability to manage the relationship with the supplier, for instance, in terms of issue handling and personality conflicts.
- Inadequate conduct of the performance, management, audit and reviews of the supplier's services.
- Unrealistic time schedules and limits attached to the supplier's responsibilities and obligations under the contract and SLA, resulting in value leakage.
- Inadequate transition planning by the organisation as the contract and SLA are implemented.
- Inadequate communication levels, both within the organisation with key personnel, and externally, with the supplier, stakeholders and end-users, through failure to develop a communications plan, assigning milestones for

16: Identifying the Risks

meetings, handling escalation procedures and periodic reviews throughout the contract.
- Inadequate information regarding the organisation's expectations regarding the project provided to the supplier.
- An inadequate retained IT department that exposes the organisation to vulnerability in the marketplace on termination of the project.
- Failure to take sufficient steps to ensure that personnel respect the need for confidentiality regarding sensitive issues.

Supplier

- Failure to be flexible during the project and allow for changes in the business environment and the needs of the organisation's end-users.
- Inadequate transition planning by the supplier as the contract and SLA are implemented.
- Lack of adequate contingency planning in the event of interruption to business or catastrophic events.
- Failure to take sufficient steps to ensure that personnel respect the need for confidentiality regarding sensitive issues.
- Failure to ensure personnel transferred to the supplier under the outsourcing contract remain motivated and committed to the project for its duration.
- Failure by the supplier to recruit adequately skilled, trained and educated personnel for implementation of the contract where the organisation's personnel are not transferred under the outsourcing contract.
- Provision of substandard or inadequate services by the supplier.

16: Identifying the Risks

Financial risks

Forecasting and identifying financial risks should occur at the outset of the project. For the organisation, a key objective of the project is to achieve business goals by increasing competitiveness, thereby increasing its profitability and benefiting shareholders and stakeholders.

It is of no value to the organisation to discover some way into the project that a key financial issue has been overlooked that significantly affects the viability of the project. In such an event, the organisation might be faced with: having to re-negotiate the contract on unfavourable terms; attempting to cancel the contract and risking heavy financial penalties or damages; or continuing performance of the contract with the expectation of significantly reduced financial returns.

Organisation

- Failure to anticipate realistic estimates of the supplier's costs and expenses, for general and customised services, including inflation and rising labour costs.
- Failure to calculate accurately the cost of resources in terms of time, skills, personnel and finance required for the development, implementation, contract management, compliance, governance and termination of the project.
- Inadequate assessment of the value of the physical and intellectual assets transferred to the supplier under the contract.
- Inadequate assessment of the financial impact of the project on the organisation before, during and after implementation, and on termination of the project.

16: Identifying the Risks

- Inadequate processes and procedures within the contract and SLA for the audit, monitoring and review of the supplier's costs and expenses throughout the project.
- Inadequate assessment of short-term cuts in cost against the long-term benefits.
- Inadequate or inaccurate calculation of cost-benefit ratios.
- Inexperienced financial personnel and advisers, lacking the necessary knowledge and negotiating skills to protect the organisation's financial interests in the tendering, pre-contract and pre-SLA stages.
- Inadequately protective penalty clauses and excessive exit costs in the contract and SLA.
- As a result of one or more of the above, value leakage.

Supplier

- Failure to control costs and expenses within the terms of the contract and the SLA.
- Inadequate financial resources to innovate and develop new systems and solutions to meet new demand from the organisation or its end-users, or to respond to changes in the business environment.
- The supplier achieving such a position of dominance during the project that the organisation is vulnerable to the supplier's request for increased charges.
- Failure of the supplier to allow for unexpected cost.
- Insolvency of the supplier or such financial difficulty that the viability of the project is prejudiced.

16: Identifying the Risks

Cloud computing risks

However apparent the benefits of the Cloud model may appear, a number of issues need consideration before an organisation commits to this business model.

A key problem is that Cloud computing is not underpinned with the formalities of a traditional IT outsourcing project. The arrangement between the parties is more casual in terms of formality and documentation. The formality of a detailed contract and SLA lend certainty to the traditional model and cement the parties' obligations and responsibilities.

Andy Ross[42], Chief Information and Technology Officer at the SHL Group, says:

> We are looking at cloud computing, but we view it with some uncertainty at the moment in terms of performance and availability. It seems a little like the Internet in the early days, rather anarchic, and we feel we need some assurance that our business needs and expectations will be met. We are particularly concerned over data security and how this can be addressed, especially where there are multi-tenants. At the moment, the existence of a standard contract and the ability to make physical checks is more reassuring.

As applies generally to any service offered over the Internet, downtime and interruption can occur, sometimes for long periods and without notice. In a situation where a supplier retains the organisation's data, interruption may involve the unavailability of data for long periods. In extreme cases, where data is lost through an interruption of service lasting several days, the organisation may find itself

---

[42] Interview: 18 June 2009.

16: Identifying the Risks

in breach of the DPA in respect of its obligations to its data subjects.

Care should be taken to ascertain the provisions of any contract governing the incidence of downtime. The outsourcing contract should include a warranty indemnifying the organisation against any claims arising from the occurrence of downtime and providing for payment of compensation; and passing the risk of any downtime on to the supplier. Any attempt by the supplier to pass this risk to the organisation may, in any event, be unreasonable under the Unfair Contract Terms Act 1977. The legal position may be further complicated where a supplier is based in a foreign jurisdiction where different legal provisions may apply.

Other problems may arise from the transmission of viruses during the Cloud computing process. The proliferation of data in close proximity in virtualised servers has the potential to enable infiltration by a wide range of malware.

While organisations may have mechanisms to prevent intrusion, these are often simply designed to support generic security issues within a firewall and will not necessarily offer the same protection to specific systems that an organisation may wish to access within the Cloud model.

There is an increasing recognition that security is a potential problem for Cloud computing. The assembly of vast amounts of data – particularly data stored on a multi-tenancy model – on remote servers is a natural attraction for cyber-criminals, who will be quick to take advantage of the absence of adequate identity management procedures.

16: Identifying the Risks

Some commentators have suggested that, as part of the due diligence process, organisations embarking on Cloud computing should insist that any prospective supplier should be subject to a security audit before, and at regular intervals during the currency of, the contract.

A related issue is that of the standards applied to the protection of data stored in the Cloud model. Typical concerns include:

- the loss of control of data to the supplier;
- the proper return of all data when required under the contract;
- the processes and procedures implemented by the supplier to ensure the organisation's data is handled securely;
- the risk of data leakage; and
- the safety of the data should the supplier become insolvent.

An emerging trend is for security to be bundled into the Cloud computing infrastructure and for security components to be included in the package offered by providers of Cloud services.

This suggests that if the Cloud market develops, providers of security solutions in the traditional model may suffer because security solutions will be embedded in Cloud services, leading to fewer, but larger, security solution providers. This bundling of security solutions into the Cloud infrastructure is referred to as 'security-as-a-service'.

Current Cloud services that are adopting this facility mainly involve the hosting of e-mail. This raises the question of the level of security offered. For e-mail that is not confidential or business-critical, a lower level of security may be

16: Identifying the Risks

acceptable than for more sensitive e-mail communications. Here, there may be an opportunity for traditional, stand-alone suppliers to offer security solutions that can be bolted on to those bundled in the Cloud infrastructure.

Conclusion

It is a sobering thought that any one of the risks identified in this chapter has the potential to bring about project failure, or impact upon the project to the extent that it is no longer worth further investment by the organisation.

To regard outsourcing as a panacea for all ills and an off-the-shelf solution is to underestimate and misunderstand fundamentally the complexity of the process. The risks surrounding the development and implementation of an IT outsourcing project are significant and substantial.

They are many and various, and they range across the strategic, technological, compliance, operational and financial functions of an organisation. For this reason, any governance must include a risk management strategy.

CHAPTER 17: RISK MANAGEMENT STRUCTURE

Assessing risk is part of the wider process of managing risk. Risk management is not simply a question of writing down procedures to ensure compliance with a set of rules, it is to ensure that prescribed procedures are observed – it is a governance function.

Not only is risk management a corporate obligation within an organisation, it is also a personal obligation of all personnel. While the strategic management of risk is a board responsibility for which the execution of its strategy may be delegated to a team of individuals, in any organisation, there must be one person ultimately accountable for the management of the organisation and its operations.

Risk management involves ascertaining, assessing and controlling potential threats and requiring all relevant personnel to take all necessary steps in managing the consequences.

Strategy principles

Some key principles must be applied in implementing a successful risk management strategy.

- First, there must be a comprehensive understanding of the scope, function and extent of the strategy, so that the correct assessment and strategy can be adopted.
- Second, there must be a culture of risk awareness, so that the temptation to disregard risk is overcome and there is

17: Risk Management Structure

an organisation-wide consciousness of the need to address risks.
- Third, the organisation must enable personnel to develop sufficient skills (including IT skills) with which to manage risks to which the organisation might be exposed.
- Fourth, the organisation must understand the range of risks to which it is vulnerable in the context of risks arising from a variety of different sources and situations, to the extent that a risk might require more than one solution for its management.
- Fifth, the organisation must be responsive to the risks brought about by a changing environment and to manage these risks as they arise. Those responsible for risk management in the organisation must be alert to the need to adapt and address new risks which may also offer new business opportunities.

Objectives and benefits

Although the immediate function of a risk management strategy is to protect the organisation against threats to its operation, there are other objectives that offer business benefits.

Risk management through efficient systems and procedures generates a culture of responsiveness to problems, particularly unexpected or enforced changes, so enabling the organisation to develop flexibility within its defined strategies.

As a result, the organisation is better positioned to take advantage of business opportunities. Its approach to the business environment becomes more confident and its

17: Risk Management Structure

willingness to extend its strategies to develop the organisation increases.

Effective risk management enables the organisation to adopt a cycle of continuous improvement. Having developed a system for devising solutions for a range of risks, the organisation develops a pattern of improved decision-making. Provided the organisation implements its risk management strategy as a continuing project, a corresponding process of continuing improvement will follow.

The combination of developing a risk management culture, agility and responsiveness in addressing risk issues, and a process of continuous improvement should enable the organisation to improve all aspects of its business performance. A comprehensive risk management strategy, effectively implemented with top-level commitment, empowers an organisation to assume complete control of its operations and to develop a positive approach to its relationships with customers and potential business opportunities.

Risk management framework

The Combined Code on Corporate Governance 2003 incorporates the original Turnbull Guidance on internal controls. Broadly, its guidance suggests that directors should review the range of risks across all functions of the organisation and identify those which it can tolerate. Next should be considered the likelihood of risks occurring, how they can be managed so their impact is minimised, and an analysis of the cost of the necessary steps for their control.

17: Risk Management Structure

In October 2005, the Financial Reporting Council published revised guidance for directors.[43] The appendix, entitled *Assessing the effectiveness of the company's risk and control processes*, identifies the following areas for guidance on risk management: risk assessment, control environment and control activities, information and communication, and monitoring.

It is clear from the appendix that internal control and risk management are the responsibility of the board and should be the subject of an annual assessment.

The risk manager

Below the board's responsibility for risk management at strategic level, will be the risk manager, who is responsible, together with a suitably qualified team, for management and execution of the strategy, including any operational risks arising during the course of the project. The risk manager has two functions.

The first is to advise the board on the risks of a particular strategy, identifying complexity, recommending tolerance thresholds and providing advice and guidance on risk handling and the application of controls.

The second is to assume 'ownership' of risks. In other words, identifying and assessing risks, maintaining risk registers and accountabilities, as well as addressing risk mitigation and any consequences for the organisation.

---

[43] *Internal Control: Revised Guidance for Directors on the Combined Code*, Financial Reporting Council, October 2005.

17: Risk Management Structure

In large organisations, the appointment of a single risk manager might be impractical, because one individual may not have the depth of knowledge and expertise to manage single-handedly the wide variety of risk to which an organisation may be exposed across all its activities; although the appointment of too many individuals runs the risk of duplication of effort or even conflict.

One solution is to treat the risk manager as a risk adviser to various line managers each of whom has responsibility for certain aspects of the organisation. For example, in terms of an outsourcing project, a contract manager might lead a contract management team in respect of the outsourcing contract, but in respect of risk management issues might take advice from the risk manager when critical 'risk' issues arise.

The risk manager must be able to take an overview, identifying strategies and objectives and selecting the most appropriate options.

The risk management team

Risk management in any organisation calls for skill and capability across a variety of different areas. In outsourcing the IT function, risk needs to be managed in the context of the strategies and operations particular to the organisation. Risks arising from development, implementation and managing the outsourcing function also require attention.

The most appropriate leader of the risk management team will be the risk manager. The risk manager must be able to articulate the advice of the team to senior management and, if necessary, to the board of directors. The risk manager must also be able to act as a channel of communication

17: Risk Management Structure

between senior management and the risk management team.

The composition of the team is critical to its success. There should certainly be at least one team member familiar with each of the risk categories identified earlier. The seniority of each team member should not be below senior management level and may well be at board level. Where there is insufficient experience of one or more of the risk areas, external consultancy may be necessary. This might arise, particularly, in the case of legal and compliance risks, where expert legal advice may be needed, both before and after a contract is signed.

The team membership should be assembled with particular qualities in mind. Members should be committed to shared and common purpose and recognise that true team membership involves a shared dependency and mutual interest in the success of a project. The team must also be capable of reacting to changes in the business environment. For example, changes required by an end-user may result in the organisation, in turn, having to re-negotiate an important part of the contract which may introduce unexpected risk issues.

The team should document its own risk control plan, or risk register, recording and rating each risk to which the outsourcing project exposes the organisation, and identifying the controls and management solutions to be applied. The risk management strategy must correspond with the business plan, goals and objectives of the organisation.

17: Risk Management Structure

Roles and responsibilities

The structure of the team should be documented, so that the framework for the management of risk is clearly understood. A documented description of the task of each team member should be available. Each member should be accountable to the risk manager, who, in turn, will be accountable to other senior management teams, perhaps the project management team and ultimately the board of directors.

Occasionally, the team may need to co-opt specific personnel to address specialist or complex risk issues, perhaps to address legal or financial issues. Depending upon the criticality of the issue, this may even be a director.

Team members should be formally inducted and informed of their respective roles and the expectations that the risk manager has of their performance. They will need ongoing training and education in awareness of new risk areas that might arise as the outsourcing project develops and proceeds to implementation.

Formal appraisal procedures will benefit not only each team member, but the team as a whole, as members' views are revealed and offer the opportunity for discussion.

Regular monitoring procedures should be in place to ensure a uniform approach to risk management – perhaps best achieved through regular reports to meetings in order to avoid team members adopting individual approaches.

Team membership should be based on the business plan of the organisation. Typically, these look ahead to the next 12 or 24 months. Within such a period, there may be significant changes in the business environment,

17: Risk Management Structure

particularly so in the area of IT. The risk management team must be responsive to actual and potential changes.

Project risk

A risk assessment will be the first task of the team. Risk assessment must take place within the scope of the project. The team can then define the scope of the risk management strategy for the outsourcing project.

Consideration must be given to the management of the project, the resources available to the team, the need for external services, and the complexity of the risks to be addressed.

Resources

The allocation of resources for the risk management team will ultimately be a decision for the board, after referral to the risk manager, senior management team and project team. Expenditure on resources can be expected to fluctuate according to the stage of the project.

Greater resources may be needed at pre-contract stage at which point key risks are being identified for management, but fewer resources may be needed once implementation has occurred as, by then, all significant risks should have been addressed.

Financial support should be provided to address all risks on an organisation-wide basis. There is little point in addressing risk departmentally. Resources should be allocated according to priorities documented by the risk management team and its risk control plan or risk register. Expenditure must be shown to offer a return on investment.

17: Risk Management Structure

The effectiveness of a strategy is not governed by the amount of expenditure, but by the effectiveness of the expenditure in meeting the firm's need.

Team functions

The objective of the team is to control, reduce or eliminate risk. Some risks are inherent. Each organisation has a different tolerance to risk and through its risk management team must decide its tolerance levels. There are three courses open to the risk management team:

- the risk might be tolerated if it is not cost-effective to manage it;
- the team can take the necessary action to eliminate the risk;
- the team can take the necessary steps to transfer the risk – most commonly undertaken by arranging insurance.

The team's strategy for managing each risk should be recorded in the risk control plan or risk register.

Risk management is, in effect, a project that takes place within a principal project, in this case, an outsourcing project. The risk management process should, therefore, be conducted in the same way as the principal project.

Records should be maintained of the different risk aspects in which the team becomes involved. The risks may vary considerably: some may involve changes in the business environment resulting in changing end-user needs; others may result from new compliance provisions; yet others may develop from unexpected difficulties with the supplier relationship.

17: Risk Management Structure

The records should show: the team member responsible; the nature of the risk; risk assessment details; details of any external assistance required; third party or stakeholder interests; the policy approved by the team; the date of senior management and project management approval; and any critical dates.

Once accepted, the risk management plan should be recorded and circulated to relevant personnel throughout the organisation. As it develops, the risk management team will collect considerable volumes of data and information which can be placed at the disposal of the organisation. This should be maintained in an ordered system as it may prove valuable for research on other occasions.

Decision processes

Once the risk control plan, or risk register, has been compiled, consideration must be given to treating the risks that have been identified. The objectives may be different according to the nature of the risk, its classification, the priority and any associated costs.

The decision process requires the team to consider the most practical solution to address the identified risks. Unless complete elimination is possible, some residual risk will remain.

Residual risk should not be confused with inherent risk. Inherent risk is critical and usually needs to be addressed as a matter of priority. The team should, therefore, give its immediate attention to inherent risk. Residual risk will require monitoring to ensure that it does not develop into inherent risk. Effectively, the degree of residual risk

17: Risk Management Structure

depends on the degree to which inherent risk can be controlled.

Implementation

Responsibility for implementation arises in two areas:

- with the risk management team, which works with the project team and is ultimately accountable to the board; and
- with those required to comply with any policies or procedures approved for introduction by the risk management team.

The risk management team has various responsibilities to fulfil in performing its function.

Incident handling

A full record of all incidents should be maintained, stating the progress and objectives in arriving at a solution. This is important, not only to cater for the absence of key personnel, but also in the provision of adequate details in the event of any claim on insurers.

Each incident should be indexed, identifying the responsible team member and a progress chart should mark the steps taken to address each risk. All those participating in the management of a particular risk should be identified, including any external consultants engaged for the purpose.

In addition, any costs incurred in the process should be recorded, so that the organisation has an idea of the ratio of the cost of the risk to the cost of its management.

17: Risk Management Structure

Action

It is important that specific authorities are obtained at the highest level, not only to signify top-level commitment, but also to ratify any action taken by the risk management team.

The level at which authority is taken will depend upon the nature and the severity of the risk for the organisation and the action recommended by the risk management team. Some actions may have significant strategic, operational or cost implications and, therefore, require authority at board level.

Monitoring

Risk management is a continuous process. As an outsourcing project proceeds, it is to be expected that the need for critical risks to be addressed recedes because such risks should have been addressed on or before the contract stage.

However, changes arise in all sorts of ways: changes in the business environment, changing demands of end-users and new legal and compliance provisions. There should, therefore, be continuous monitoring by the risk management team both to ensure that any new risks that arise are adequately addressed, and to check that measures taken to address existing risks remain effective.

Monitoring risk management has a number of functions:

- to test the effectiveness of existing solutions; and
- to check the extent a risk has been addressed as planned.

There should be regular, formally recorded monitoring meetings with reports from those responsible for each risk

17: Risk Management Structure

area and a formal evaluation process, with records of any change to risk profiles and the adoption of new solutions.

Audit

An audit process is essential to ensure the risk management team is performing to the standards required by the organisation. An organisation may select internal or external controls according to the complexity and nature of the risk and any solutions adopted.

Risk management standards

The BSI has developed a Code of Practice, BS 31100:2008[44], for risk management. This provides recommendations for the framework, process and implementation of risk management. It is designed for: 'CEOs, CFOs, CROs, CIOs, COOs and CTOs; chairmen and company secretaries; managing, finance and IT directors and risk managers', among a number of other categories.

Its perspectives include:

- business objectives;
- proactive risk management;
- risk management oversight; and
- stakeholders' interests.

BSI has also published principles and guidelines for implementation for BS 31100. At the time of writing, the

---

[44] Permission to reproduce from BS 31100:2008 is granted by BSI (see p.271).

17: Risk Management Structure

BSI website stated that a draft had been published for consultation on 12 May 2008, with an expiry date of 31 July 2008.

It is likely that a final version will shortly be available and regular monitoring is advisable.

The National Institute of Standards and Technology (NIST)[45] (*www.nist.gov*) has published a guide: *Risk Management Guide for Information Technology Systems* (July 2002). Its introduction states that risk management is not a technical IT process, but 'an essential management function of the organisation'.

Risk management technology

There are large numbers of software solutions in the IT marketplace claiming to create and manage the documentation required for effective risk assessment and risk management processes.

The main difficulty for the organisation lies in deciding which solution is most appropriate to meet its needs. The problem is compounded by the fact that there seems to be no overriding benchmark quality standard which provides any differentiation for the unsuspecting organisation.

To give an idea of the types of solution that are available, the solutions of two providers are summarised below. Further details of each are available at their respective websites. They are not an endorsement of the particular

---

[45] *Risk Management Guide for Information Technology Systems*: Special Publication 800-30, Stoneburger G, Goguen A and Feringa A, National Institute of Standards and Technology, July 2002.

17: Risk Management Structure

solution. They are suggested simply as an example of where to look next for ideas on how IT can assist in the overall risk management process.

Risk Reasoning[46]

This solution is intended for the management of risk in respect of all activities of an organisation, from projects and programmes to corporate strategy. *RiskAid* is designed to help users adopt a logical process when identifying and quantifying risks and developing solutions that either eliminate or mitigate its effects.

The solution providers claim that this program was the first risk management tool to be accredited by APMG-UK[47] a leading accreditation, certification and qualification organisation recognised by government agencies.

RiskAid Enterprise has been developed beyond the project management specification of *RiskAid* and offers more comprehensive support for organisations. This comprises a unified risk management framework which can be applied throughout an organisation at all levels.

Risk Reasoning's website helpfully provides screenshots of the key steps of the risk management process, for instance, prioritising, developing an action plan, assessment summaries, a risk register and a risk matrix.

---

[46] www.riskreasoning.co.uk
[47] www.apmgroup.co.uk

17: Risk Management Structure

Pentana Ltd[48]

Pentana Audit Work Systems (PAWS) is designed to address governance and assurance needs and integrates risk management and internal controls, so that risk management and compliance issues can be addressed. Web-based modules enable direct update of risks, controls and audits.

Retain Resource Planning Software is designed to help optimise the use and availability of resources, for instance, consultants, and additional modules address time recording, skills selection and links to project management solutions.

Pentana's website provides a schedule of the components of each module for easier understanding of its function.

Conclusion

The risks to be managed in an IT outsourcing project are many and various, but all have the potential to have a profound impact on the project.

A formal risk management framework is essential for two reasons:

- the complexity of the implications of many of the risks, especially those involving compliance issues; and
- their potential impact on the organisation if they are not adequately managed.

Having considered the construction of a risk management framework, the next step is to consider some strategic approaches to managing the risks arising in an outsourcing project.

---

[48] *www.pentana.com*

CHAPTER 18: RISK MANAGEMENT STRATEGIES

A key requirement of good governance is the effective management of risk. Effective management of risk goes to the heart of successfully applying and implementing governance principles. This chapter considers strategies and mechanisms that support organisations in the introduction, application and implementation of governance principles in managing the risks of an outsourcing project.

The chapter returns to the familiar analysis and examines: IT, compliance, operational and financial mechanisms available to organisations embarking on a project concerned with outsourcing the IT function.

Management of IT risks

In recent years, various frameworks and standards have emerged to support organisations in their use and management of IT. In the context of outsourcing, they will have limited impact on the organisation because the IT function is being outsourced to a supplier.

However, in terms of managing the IT risks of outsourcing, the standards are of considerable significance. They are benchmarks by which an organisation can make an assessment of a supplier's credentials and suitability for performing its obligations under an outsourcing contract.

Every organisation is different and some standards may be more appropriate to the proposed outsourcing project than others. The absence of certification of a supplier in respect of the proposed services may not be fatal in the tendering

18: Risk Management Strategies

process, but from the perspective of managing risk, a prudent organisation will surely prefer a supplier able to provide evidence of certification to recognised management standards relevant to performance of the project. It is important to understand the status of the various standards, codes and specifications available.

The International Accreditation Forum[49] is an international association of national accreditation bodies, one of which is the United Kingdom Accreditation Service (UKAS), which focuses on setting standards across a wide range of management functions.

In the United Kingdom, UKAS[50] is the national accreditation body which accredits UK organisations, such as the British Standards Institution (BSI), for the provision of audit and certification services. British standards are identified by the prefix BS; international standards, by the prefix ISO; and European standards, by the prefix EN.

BSI is accredited to provide certification services to organisations seeking to achieve compliance with any of the numerous standards that now abound across all areas of commerce, industry and government. The International Electro-technical Commission is another standards body and its acronym, IEC, is often a prefix to a standard.

Standards are often supported by codes of practice. Compliance with these codes supports compliance with a standard, but is not treated as conclusive evidence of compliance; and it is possible for organisations to achieve certification under a particular standard without necessarily

---

[49] www.iaf.nu
[50] www.ukas.com

18: Risk Management Strategies

adopting the relevant code of practice. Codes of practice should be regarded as guidance upon best practice – in other words 'should' not 'shall'. They are not obligatory and, as such, cannot be audited for certification.

PAS is a Publicly Available Specification against which audit and certification is possible. Sometimes certification is possible against an individual specification, while other specifications are embodied in larger standards.

This section considers five areas of IT where recognised standards and industry codes may be relevant in the assessment of a supplier's suitability as a candidate for outsourcing.

Asset management

PAS 55 1: 2008: Asset management. Specification for the optimised management of physical assets

Where they are being transferred under an outsourcing contract, the organisation needs assurance that assets and asset systems will be managed optimally and sustainably. This standard specifies the requirements for an asset management system for the management of physical assets and asset systems over their life cycle. The standard applies to all sizes of organisation.

PAS 55 2:2008: Asset management. Guidelines for the application of PAS 55-1

This provides guidance on understanding the requirements of PAS 55-1:2008 and on establishment, implementation, maintenance, and improvement of asset management systems. It does not prescribe mandatory approaches.

18: Risk Management Strategies

ISO/IEC 19770-1:2006: Software asset management

This standard certifies that an organisation applies corporate governance requirements to the management of software assets and IT service management. An organisation that includes the transfer of software assets to a supplier as part of an outsourcing project might wish to include certification to this standard as a condition of contracting with a prospective supplier.

The standard also has potential as a risk management tool and other benefits include the monitoring of cost and the offer of a competitive advantage.

Service provision

ISO/IEC 20000-1:2005 and ISO/IEC 20000-2:2005

This standard defines the requirements for a service provider to deliver managed services.

It is suggested for consideration by businesses tendering for their services, for a consistent approach by suppliers in a supply chain, as a benchmark for service management, as the basis for an independent assessment, as a means of demonstrating an ability to meet customer requirements, and as a means of improving service standards.

Part 1 of the standard comprises the specification and Part 2 is a supporting code of conduct.

18: Risk Management Strategies

Business continuity

BS 25999-1:2006: Business continuity: code of practice

BS 25999-2:2007: Business continuity: specification

These standards represent, respectively, the code of practice and the specification for business continuity. The code provides a comprehensive set of controls based on best practice throughout the business continuity management life cycle.

The standard specifies the requirements for establishing, implementing, monitoring, reviewing, exercising, maintaining and improving a documented business continuity plan. The standard does not seek to impose uniformity, rather for organisations to develop strategies for their needs.

BS 25777:2008: Information and communications technology continuity management: code of practice

This code of practice is intended to support a wider business continuity plan and addresses the subset of information and communications technology (ICT). The code covers such issues as: ICT continuity programme management; ICT continuity strategies and their development, implementation exercising, testing, maintenance, review and improvement.

The code supports the process towards certification under *BS 25999-2:2007: Specification for business continuity management.*

18: Risk Management Strategies

ISO/IEC 24762:2008: Information technology. Security techniques: Guidelines for information and communications technology disaster recovery services

This standard offers guidance on the provision of disaster recovery services as part of business continuity management. The standard is expressed as especially suited to outsourced service providers as it describes the best practices that suppliers should consider. It highlights specialist requirements, such as special encryption software and secured operation procedures, equipment, knowledgeable personnel and application documentation.

Information security

ISO/IEC 27001: Information security

This standard provides a benchmark for the management of information security management systems. It is expressed as being most effective for supplier organisations which manage information on behalf of other organisations as it can be used to assure organisations that their data is properly protected.

There are also a number of other standards addressing the management of information security issues. They include:

- ISO/IEC 27005:2008: Information security techniques.
- ISO/IEC 27002:2005: Information technology security techniques: code of practice.
- ISO/IEC TR 14516:2002: Information technology security techniques: guidelines for use and management by trusted third parties.
- ISO/IEC 27004: Information security techniques: information security management: measurement.

18: Risk Management Strategies

Data protection

BS 10012:2009[51]: Specification for a personal information management system

Data protection issues involve both technology and compliance issues. A British standard has been published specifying the requirements for a personal information management system. It provides an infrastructure that includes the implementation of a framework for compliance with the DPA.

It is intended for adoption by organisations of any size and provides a framework for managing personal data that meets compliance standards of both internal and external audits.

GAISP

GAISP is a project concerning Generally Accepted Security Principles and is an attempt to develop a cohesive approach from information security professionals against a background of a multitude of fragmented approaches towards information security.

The aim of the project is to establish a set of commonly accepted good practices for information security throughout industry, commerce and governments, globally.

---

[51] Permission to reproduce extracts from the British Standards quoted on pages 188, 214, 261 and 267-271 is granted by BSI. British Standards can be obtained in PDF or hard copy formats from the BSI online shop: *www.bsigroup.com/Shop* or by contacting BSI Customer Services for hardcopies only: telephone: +44 (0)20 8996 9001, e-mail: *cservices@bsigroup.com*.

18: Risk Management Strategies

Further details are available from the website of Information System Auditing Resources (*www.securityprocedures.com/principles-generally-accepted-information-security-principles-gaisp*).

Governance

The principles of CobiT in respect of IT governance were discussed earlier. Observance and adoption of the principles are an important strategy for the management of risks arising from IT outsourcing.

They are principles with which every supplier of outsourced IT services should be familiar. An organisation outsourcing its IT function should ensure at tendering stage that a prospective supplier recognises the philosophy of CobiT.

The set of principles developed by ITIL considered earlier, is concerned with the quality of service provision and offers a life cycle model for the management of IT service provision. Ensuring a supplier's observation of the ITIL principles should help protect the organisation from inadequate service provision.

Cloud computing

The Jericho Forum[52] has produced some useful research into this issue and advises that organisations need to categorise the different types of risk that Cloud computing poses when deciding the volume of services an organisation

---

[52] *Cloud Cube Model version 1*, Jericho Forum, April 2009, available at: *www.opengroup.org*.

18: Risk Management Strategies

can commit to the Cloud. The Jericho Forum model identifies different types of Cloud model:

- Open/proprietary
- Perimiterised/de-perimiterised
- Internal/external.

These models are applied to five types of service, or layers, for which Cloud computing might be appropriate:

- Infrastructure
- Platform
- Software
- Process
- Outcome/value.

Different security considerations are needed for each permutation. Identity and access issues also arise, together with the potential for legal and jurisdictional problems in the event of legal disputes. Cloud computing raises particular security issues as it involves multi-tenants through virtualisation of data servers. This means that the data of numerous organisations may be stored in one compartmentalised server. There are considerable security risks to the data of any of the 'tenant' organisations.

In April 2009, the Cloud Security Alliance[53] published guidance on managing security issues in Cloud computing. In its introduction, the report states:

We do see cloud computing as being a major change coming to every business; as information security practitioners, we

---

[53] *Security Guidance for Critical Areas of Focus in Cloud Computing,* CSA Cloud Computing Alliance, April 2009, *www.cloudsecurityalliance.org.*

18: Risk Management Strategies

recognise that there are verities which must not change good governance, managing risks and common sense. Cloud computing is an unstoppable force and we encourage security practitioners to lead, help and accelerate its secure adoption aided by common sense, rather than standing on the sidelines and letting business move forward without us.

The guidance proposes 15 'domains' in which security issues need to be addressed:

- Cloud computing architectural framework;
- governance and enterprise risk management;
- legal;
- electronic discovery;
- compliance and audit;
- information lifecycle management;
- portability and interoperability;
- traditional security, business continuity and disaster recovery;
- data centre operations;
- incident response, notification and remediation;
- application security;
- encryption and key management;
- identity and access management;
- storage; and
- virtualisation.

This is a comprehensive report for which the compilers are to be commended. It is required reading for organisations contemplating the outsourcing of its IT function on this model, and also as a resource for suppliers wishing to anticipate and address organisations' concerns.

18: Risk Management Strategies

Some solutions are beginning to emerge. Commensus[54] has developed its Virtual Infrastructure Platform (C-VIP) which claims to offer a secure solution for data stored and compartmentalised in virtualised servers.

IT service provision

In terms of exposure to risks arising from IT services, there is a wide variety of issues on which the organisation should seek confirmation of adequate performance from the supplier, for example:

- Management information:
    o records of past performance levels;
    o records of forecast performance levels; and
    o IT systems and server management records.
- Compliance:
    o evidence of ability to comply with the contract;
    o evidence of ability to comply with the SLA;
    o evidence of compliance with any relevant standards and methodologies; and
    o proposals for compliance audits.
- Security:
    o security of servers;
    o security of networks;
    o security of IT platforms and infrastructure;
    o security of applications;
    o application of intrusion detection and prevention systems; and

---

[54] www.commensus.com

18: Risk Management Strategies

- o application of encryption technology and standards applied.
- Performance:
  - o procedures for monitoring the service;
  - o procedures for reviewing the service; and
  - o reviews of metrics and service levels.

No matter how thoroughly due diligence procedures are undertaken, the organisation can never be certain of the quality of the supplier's performance until operations begin. An organisation should be as rigorous as possible in its assessment of a Cloud supplier before the contract begins.

Management of legal and compliance risks

Certification to a benchmark standard and conformity with industry standards prescribe best practice. Best practice must be supported by compliance with relevant legal and regulatory provisions. Compliance is a critical risk management issue for the board of any organisation intent on outsourcing its IT function.

Data Protection Act 1998

The object of outsourcing the IT function is that an experienced supplier should provide a service that meets the requirements of the organisation more efficiently than the organisation's in-house IT function. Outsourcing an IT function will almost inevitably involve the supplier processing the organisation's data in some way.

The DPA provides a framework for the management of personal data. While the DPA contains the legal provisions, it does not prescribe procedures. The manner of compliance

18: Risk Management Strategies

is a decision for each organisation. The organisation must decide on a case-by-case basis how to ensure the supplier complies with the DPA according to its business strategy.

Data protection principles

Eight data protection principles are set out in the DPA.

- Data must be processed fairly and lawfully.
- Personal data may only be processed for certain purposes and not for any other incompatible reasons.
- Data processed must be adequate, relevant and not excessive in relation to the reason for processing.
- Data must be up to date and accurate.
- Data must not be stored longer than necessary.
- Data must be processed in recognition of the rights of those whose information is stored.
- There must be appropriate technical and organisational measures against unauthorised processing of, or loss or damage to, personal data.
- Data must not be transferred outside the EEA without adequately protecting the individual's rights.

The Information Commissioner administers the DPA and codes of practice and guidance notes are on the website.[55] The DPA establishes three categories of data handler.

The *data controller* decides the purpose and manner of the processing of the personal data in question. The *data processor* is a person, other than an employee of the data controller, who processes data on behalf of the data

---

[55] www.ico.gov.uk.

18: Risk Management Strategies

controller. The *data subject* is the individual whose personal data is processed.

In the outsourcing process, it is most likely that the organisation will be the data controller, and the supplier will be the data processor, with the organisation's end-users being data subjects. However, the roles of data controller and data processor can overlap and the data controller and data processor can be the same person.

The key issue for the organisation to understand is that, even though its data is transferred to the supplier, nonetheless, the organisation remains responsible as data controller or data processor for the data being handled in accordance with the eight DPA principles.

Personal data is data that relates to a living individual who can be identified from the data alone, or from that data and any other information either in the possession, or likely to come into the possession, of the data controller. Stringent provisions govern the handling of data defined as sensitive by the DPA, such as personnel or medical records. Any doubts over the nature of any data being processed should be referred to the Information Commissioner for guidance, and if necessary, legal advice should be obtained.

Non-compliance

The DPA provides that non-compliance carries certain criminal sanctions. For minor infringements, the Information Commissioner can accept undertakings for steps to be taken to prevent future breaches.

In more serious cases, criminal proceedings may be taken and, on conviction before either a magistrates' court or the Crown Court, are punishable with a fine. There are also

18: Risk Management Strategies

supplementary penalties of destruction or erasure of any data that is being unlawfully processed. Other remedies include enforcement notices and forfeiture proceedings.

Under the DPA, unless exempt, a data controller commits a criminal offence by processing personal data without first having registered with (the official term is to 'notify') the Information Commissioner. Although criminal proceedings may not always follow, in more serious cases the Information Commissioner will take action. For instance, in the last two years, the Information Commissioner has prosecuted a number of firms of solicitors for failure to notify.

Under the DPA, criminal offences can be committed by the following:

- the data controller;
- corporate officers of the data controller, such as a director, manager or company secretary (where there is evidence of connivance or neglect);
- employees of the data controller; and
- any individual aiding and abetting an offence under the DPA.

The Information Commissioner's website publishes details of proceedings for non-compliance.

Criminal sanctions are not the only consequences for failure to comply with the DPA. A data security breach or publicity arising from illegally processing data may have two further consequences.

First, the data subject may pursue a claim for damages for negligence for either breach of contract or negligent breach of an implied duty to take reasonable care to ensure the

18: Risk Management Strategies

security and confidentiality of any data held by the data controller.

Second, there is the potential for significant damage to the data controller's reputation arising from publicity over a breach of the DPA, as well as any criminal proceedings.

Third parties

An IT outsourcing project invariably involves the use of the organisation's data for the provision of services by a supplier. In such cases, the outsourcing contract should contain a provision that the supplier, as data processor, is obliged to process any relevant personal data:

- in accordance with the instructions of the organisation (as data controller); and
- in compliance with each principle of the DPA; but particularly principle seven which addresses the security and confidentiality of personal data.

Where a supplier proceeds to process any personal data held by the organisation, it must do so with the clear instructions of the organisation, otherwise the organisation may be committing an offence under section 55 of the DPA.

Under this section, knowingly or recklessly disclosing personal data to another person without the consent of the data controller is an offence unless:

- necessary for the prevention or detection of crime;
- required by law;
- with reasonable belief that the disclosure was legal;
- with reasonable belief that the data controller (the organisation) would have consented.

18: Risk Management Strategies

This provision applies to any sub-contracting and successive sub-contracting of the outsourcing project by the supplier. The outsourcing contract should, therefore, contain an overarching provision that only data processing specifically authorised by the organisation as data controller can be undertaken.

International data transfers

In some circumstances, the organisation may decide to outsource its IT function to a supplier who is based abroad. There are strict provisions in the DPA governing the management of personal data outside the United Kingdom.

Principle eight of the DPA states:

Personal data shall not be transferred to a country or territory outside the European Economic Area unless that country or territory ensures an adequate level of protection for the rights and freedoms of data subjects in relation to the processing of personal data.

The Information Commissioner has expressed the view that the mere transit through technical routing of personal data through a country beyond the EEA and for which an EEA country is its final destination may not breach the principle. In other words, mere transit may not breach the principle. There must be some recognisable act of acceptance by the third country.

The key words of the principle are 'adequate level of protection' and the criteria for meeting this requirement. The DPA (schedule I, part II, paragraph 13) suggests the following criteria:

- the nature of the data;
- the reason for, and the duration of the processing;

18: Risk Management Strategies

- the country of origin and country of final destination;
- the rules of law of the third country; and
- the professional rules and security measures in the third country.

The Information Commissioner issued guidance in this area in December 2008[56] which contains suggestions on how to approach the problem of international data transfers outside the European Economic Area.

Special provisions also govern the transfer of personal data to the United States of America. The Safe Harbor Principles set out the criteria for data transfer as below.

- The organisation must inform the data subject of the reasons for collecting data; to whom the data will be ßdisclosed; and the processing controls to be applied.
- Data subjects must have the right to opt out of the proposed transfer.
- Data must not be transferred to another country unless it is a Safe Harbor subscriber, subject to the EU Data Protection Directive, or subject to another approved agreement.
- Adequate data protection policies must be in place regarding disclosure, protection and destruction of information.
- Data must be processed in accordance with the first principle of the DPA.

---

[56] *Data Protection Act 1998: the eighth data protection principle and international data transfers*, ICO, December 2008, available at: *www.ico.gov.uk/upload/documents/library/data_protection/detailed_s pecialist_guides/international_transfers_legal_guidance_v3.0_171208. pdf.*

18: Risk Management Strategies

- Data subjects must have a right to access their data and to correct errors.
- A complaints and dispute resolution procedure must be published.

In respect of data transfers to other countries, model contractual clauses have been developed specifically to address these requirements. Some details of these can be found at the website of the International Chamber of Commerce (www.iccwbo.org).

The provisions concerning data transfer to countries outside the EEA are complex and may be subject to different applicable laws and jurisdictions. In all such circumstances, legal advice should be obtained to ensure compliance with the relevant provisions governing the proposed data transfer and that the contract is appropriate.

BS 10012:2009: Specification for a personal information management system

This standard offers an infrastructure for the management of personal information management systems that accords with best practice principles and provides compliance with the DPA for organisations of any size.

Cloud computing

Outsourcing in the Cloud environment calls for special consideration to be given to the managing of the risk to an organisation's data. An organisation needs to ask: where its data is going; in whose possession it will be; who might be sharing it; and what provision there is for it being ring-fenced. Particular regard should be paid to including

18: Risk Management Strategies

provisions in the contract to protect the organisation's vulnerability to infringement of the DPA. The organisation should address such issues as:

- any other parties who may be able to access data stored in virtualised servers;
- any other jurisdictions that may be involved;
- the adequacy of any security policies to protect its data;
- the supplier's compliance with any relevant legislative and regulatory provisions regarding data-handling;
- the authority, competence, qualification and availability of the supplier's personnel in handling the organisation's data;
- evidence of provision for disaster recovery and business continuity.

The organisation should take whatever steps are necessary to ensure that its data will be no less secure from physical or technological interference in the supplier's possession as it would be if it had been retained by the organisation.

This may involve various intrusive enquiries, such as sight of the supplier's data security policies; reservation of the right to audit the supplier's systems; sight of the security qualifications and employment records of the supplier's personnel; verification of any security standards with which the supplier has been accredited.

The provisions of the DPA apply equally in Cloud computing outsourcing as to the traditional outsourcing model. Virtualised data servers enable numerous organisations' data to be transferred worldwide, seamlessly and unobtrusively without any knowledge on the part of an organisation. The organisation is responsible for any movement of its data across jurisdictions.

18: Risk Management Strategies

Alistair Maughan[57], outsourcing specialist partner in law firm, Morrison & Foerster, makes the point that the traditional model is far more certain in concept than the Cloud model which is ephemeral. In this model, he suggests, there is a shift in dynamics with the organisation moving towards conformity with the supplier's business environment, whereas the position is reversed in the traditional model.

The Cloud environment may involve data passing through numerous jurisdictions. In such cases, the organisation should obtain specialist legal advice on the specific requirements that must be observed to achieve compliance.

Copyright Design and Patents Act 1988

Where an IT outsourcing project involves the transfer of software developed by the organisation to the supplier, the provisions of the CDPA may require consideration. The issues that arise in such a situation were considered earlier, in connection with the terms and provisions of the outsourcing contract.

The CDPA gives creators of certain types of work the right to protect the manner in which their work is used and, where it is used, for permission to be obtained beforehand.

Copyright applies to original work which demonstrates the application of skill, thought and labour. There is no copyright in an idea. Copyright arises from the manner in which a particular idea is explained.

---

[57] Interview: 18 May 2009.

18: Risk Management Strategies

The categories of work included by the CDPA cover literary work, which includes computer programs. Normally, the creator of the software will have exclusive right to take legal proceedings in the event of a possible infringement, although an exception arises where the software is developed by an individual acting as an employee, or perhaps an independent contractor who has contracted that the rights in any software developed under a contract remains with the organisation.

The law of copyright is complex, especially in the context of software development where variations of original programs frequently obscure its origins, so that compliance with the CDPA is problematic.

Care must, therefore, be taken at contract stage to ensure that the provisions of the CDPA are observed and that the origins of any software to be included in the outsourcing contract are correctly identified, so that the appropriate licences are obtained.

In most IT outsourcing projects, the measures needed to comply with the CDPA will invariably require legal advice and assistance. This is to ensure that, not only are all the required licences obtained for the intended use, but also that the supplier's use of the software, and the use by any parties to whom the supplier may subcontract its services to perform the contract, is limited to the scope of the project.

Transfer of Undertaking (Protection of Employment) Regulations 2006

These apply to the transfer of undertakings, or part of an undertaking, and are intended to protect the rights of

18: Risk Management Strategies

transferred personnel by securing the same terms and conditions as if employed by the original undertaking.

TUPE 2006 implements three EC Directives:

- Acquired Rights Directive (77/187/EC);
- Acquired Rights Directive (98/50/EC); and
- Acquired Rights Amendment Directive (2001/23/EC).

TUPE 2006 applies to service provision where services are outsourced, in-sourced, or assigned to a new contractor. The objective is to make the contractor aware of the rights of transferred personnel.

TUPE 2006 applies to business transfers and service provision where an undertaking is a 'stable economic entity'. It has no need to be profit-making and applies where an identifiable part is transferred. Factors to consider are: whether the transferor's business is the same as the transferee's business; whether there has been a transfer of tangible assets; whether customers have been transferred; whether the majority of employees have been taken over by the transferee. If, on balance, the answer is in the affirmative, there is, arguably, a stable economic entity.

TUPE 2006 will usually apply to the contracting out of services, but does not apply to: the transfer of shares on a take-over; the transfer of assets only; transfer of a contract for goods and services if personnel are not involved; the supply of goods; and transfers outside the UK, although there may be similar provisions in another jurisdiction.

In deciding whether a dismissal after a transfer is fair, specific legal advice should be sought, but as a general rule: a dismissal for which the transfer is the dominant reason will be unfair; a dismissal for a reason related to the transfer may be unfair under the 'reasonable' test under

18: Risk Management Strategies

employment legislation; a dismissal for a reason unrelated to the transfer is not caught by TUPE 2006.

Under the provisions of TUPE 2006, the transferor must give prescribed information about the rights of any personnel to the transferee. Failure to do so entitles the transferee to apply to a tribunal for minimum compensation of £500 per employee. There are also provisions governing consultation and notification to employees.

TUPE 2006 does not govern the transfer of pensions, but the Pensions Act 2004 applies to transfers after 6 April 2005 and contains similar provisions in respect of pension rights.

Personnel employed with the transferor for less than a period of one year have no protection under TUPE 2006.

If personnel are being outsourced, the organisation should obtain: confirmation in the contract that adequately skilled and resourced personnel will be allocated to the project; a right of veto over the employment of certain personnel on reasonable grounds; and an assurance that there will be continuity so as to avoid frequent need to train replacements. The provisions are complex, especially where large numbers of personnel are included in the outsourcing project and specialist legal advice should be taken to ensure compliance.

Summary

Compliance is one of the most concerning issues for an organisation engaged in an IT outsourcing project. The key compliance provisions are complex and will invariably require specialist legal advice. In addition, the pace of development in the area of legal and regulatory compliance

18: Risk Management Strategies

means that keeping up to date with the relevant legislation is both difficult and time-consuming.

However, in the context of creating and maintaining a framework of good governance, allocating resources (in terms of training personnel and relying upon legal expertise) for the management of compliance risk is essential. Organisations that underestimate the importance of compliance issues do so at their peril.

Management of operational risks

A contract for the procurement of outsourced services is not the conclusion of the project. The project does not end when the contract is signed – that is when the project begins. Three critical factors in achieving success will be:

- how the organisation manages the changes brought about by outsourcing its IT function;
- where the contract provides for the organisation's personnel to be included in the outsourcing project, how the supplier manages the organisation's personnel; and
- how the organisation manages its relationship with the supplier throughout the project.

These factors interact with each other and a full understanding of the interaction between them is necessary if the outsourcing project is to prosper.

Change management

Methodical and carefully planned change is more likely to succeed than change brought about by crisis management. As every organisation is different, so the process of change will differ.

18: Risk Management Strategies

Before the contract stage, it is important to take account of comments from personnel who have regular contact with customers and strategic allies of the organisation. Outsourcing will bring no benefit to the organisation if the proposal alienates customers or agencies upon whose goodwill the organisation depends.

Implementing change involves ensuring acceptance by all those who are affected by the proposals. An inclusive approach is required for this and an ability to take a broad view of the project. Personnel must become used to new ideas and performance standards. Change of almost any description will bring about resistance in some quarters and can result in anxiety and stress.

There are different types of change:

- Progressive change
- Recurring change
- Dictated change
- Shared change.

An IT outsourcing project will involve dictated change introduced by the board but may also involve shared change (with the supplier) and progressive change as the project develops.

Change needs to be planned. Detailed implementation plans should be developed and circulated to all personnel concerned. The plan should give a chronological outline of the steps to be taken and assign roles and responsibilities. The effects should be discussed with those most affected as they are likely to have a greater understanding of the impact on their positions.

A convenient approach to change may be the adoption of one or more of three methods:

18: Risk Management Strategies

- a time-based trial for a short period to identify and correct difficulties before the project formally begins;
- a pilot project, manned by volunteers, to eradicate any defects in the project plan;
- staged implementation – a strategy that is useful where personnel need to acquire new skills as the project develops; this approach also enables control to be exercised as the changes are small quantities.

A key factor in successfully managing change is the provision of timely and relevant information to ensure adequate awareness and understanding of the aims and objectives of the project.

Outsourcing the IT function

Where the outsourcing project involves the outsourcing of simply the IT function, with the supplier providing the personnel required to perform the contract, there will be a significant impact on personnel within the organisation's IT department.

Consideration will need to be given to relevant employment protection legislation to ensure that appropriate consultation processes take place and redundancy payments and remuneration packages are accurately calculated and promptly paid.

The disappearance of traditional posts associated with an in-house IT department, such as procurement, support, maintenance and budgeting, may mean that the IT function of the organisation effectively disappears.

The constitution of the organisation's retained IT department was considered earlier.

18: Risk Management Strategies

Outsourcing personnel

Where the outsourcing project involves the outsourcing of both the IT function and its own personnel in order to perform the contract, there are similar, but different, considerations. The reconstituted IT department will be required to operate in whatever format is appropriate for ensuring that IT features of the project are addressed in line with the business goals of the organisation.

However, it is in the interests of the organisation that the supplier inherits and manages a team of personnel willing and able to perform to an adequate standard. The organisation will, therefore, be concerned that:

- transferred personnel are required to maintain high standards of confidentiality;
- transferred personnel are provided with adequate and appropriate training, education and opportunities for new skills development;
- when necessary, replacement personnel of a suitable standard of skill and expertise are recruited;
- adequate communication channels operate between the supplier's management team and new personnel;
- the supplier should engender a culture of teamwork so as to avoid the risk of demoralisation of any transferred personnel;
- the supplier takes whatever steps are necessary to ensure that differences of culture with the organisation are identified and managed.

The Investors in People standard is the most widely applied 'people' standard. It is a national standard which prescribes training and development levels for personnel to achieve

18: Risk Management Strategies

organisational goals. The organisation should consider whether this standard should be adopted by the supplier.

Andy Ross[58] of SHL Group says:

> One of SHL's major concerns was that outsourced personnel should feel that the future with our supplier was secure. They were kept informed of developments on a regular basis. Some saw the transfer as an opportunity and, later during the contract, others returned to work with us. We selected a site that was close to our offices, so that our personnel did not feel they were undervalued.

One of the key concerns of the organisation will be that, in the pursuit of a more profitable return under the contract, the supplier may seek to replace inherited personnel with less costly staff with fewer skills. Constant personnel changes and engagement of replacements with inadequately skilled personnel place an outsourcing project at risk. If the project does not yield an adequate return on investment, outsourcing is not viable. Again, the attitude of a supplier to achieving Investors in People certification might be evidence of how a supplier views personnel and is an issue that could be raised during the tendering process.

Managing the supplier relationship

Managing the SLA relationship was considered earlier. If the outsourcing project is to succeed, any relationship with the supplier must succeed in all aspects of the project.

---

[58] Interview: 18 June 2009.

18: Risk Management Strategies

Tim Amatt, Project Director at EquaTerra[59], says that the nature of the relationship and how it is managed can depend on the business model.

He suggests there are three key alternatives:

- Transactional: being commodity-based, with a focus on cost where any supplier can deliver the service and the need for a close relationship is less necessary.
- Collaborative: where there is a measure of interdependence between the parties; a requirement for mutual trust and an understanding of each other's business; and greater reliance on one another in the process and delivery.
- True partnership: which may typically be a joint venture, with common objectives, shared risks and mutual benefit – perhaps the least common outsourcing business model.

In the first business model, the relationship can be more perfunctory. It may succeed or fail on the price, performance of the contract and SLA as this is the dominant issue for both parties.

In the second and third models, other issues are of far greater importance, such as mutual trust, shared risks and an understanding of the parties' respective businesses. Here, the relationship will need to be on a much deeper level as the organisations are much more intertwined by their respective dependencies. The governance structures to support this need to be developed to a far greater extent to reflect the strategic nature of the relationship.

---

[59] Interview: 23 June 2009.

18: Risk Management Strategies

There are three types of processes at work when managing relationships with a supplier of outsourced services: formal processes, business processes and informal processes.

Formal processes

These types of process are governed by the formal documentation that constitutes the whole contract for the outsourcing project.

The contract and SLA establish the terms on which the project is performed. The terms of each should be clearly expressed and understood, so that both parties have a mutually agreed understanding of each other's respective expectations.

In complex outsourcing projects, representatives of both organisation and supplier should be given training in the content and implications of key terms of the contract.

Corporate, IT and project governance principles and frameworks formalise board, management executive and administrative functions. The organisation must strive to observe and apply these principles throughout.

Business processes

Behaviour that brings about mutual understanding and co-operation helps cement relationships. Examples include:

- identifying and sharing mutual objectives;
- transparency throughout the project;
- confidentiality whenever required;
- a full understanding of each other's expectations;
- adequate communication channels;

- appropriate and proportionate provision of resources by each party in the performance of the contract;
- standardisation of processes to avoid complexity and potential disputes;
- adequate levels of supervision at key stages of the project; and
- regular consultation and feedback from end-users.

Informal processes

Informal processes add a personal element to the project. They are the trust, value and personal empathy between key personnel from both organisation and supplier – behaviour which makes each party feel comfortable with the dealings between them.

During an outsourcing project, an organisation entrusts its IT function to a supplier of whom it may not have heard before the tendering process. Even if financial proposals of one supplier are less favourable, preference might be given to a supplier with whom the organisation feels there is likely to be mutual trust, mutual respect for values and some personal empathy at board, management and executive levels.

Management of financial risks

Financial issues arise in three further areas: legal and compliance, contractual issues and audit procedures.

18: Risk Management Strategies

Legal and compliance provisions

The two key compliance provisions addressing financial risks are the Sarbanes-Oxley Act 2002 and Basel practice guidance.

Sarbanes-Oxley Act 2002

This Act applies to publicly listed companies, management and public accountancy firms in the USA, together with UK subsidiaries of these organisations, provided the holding company has a significant interest and influence over the internal controls and profitability of the subsidiary. The Act does not apply to private companies.

Organisations are categorised by: 'large accelerated filers' with a worldwide market value of over $700 million; 'accelerated filers' with worldwide market value of over $75 million but less than $700 million; and 'non-accelerated filers' comprising small companies.

On 23 May 2007, the Securities and Exchange Commission issued guidance to non-accelerated filers (*Sarbanes Oxley (SOX) Compliance, SOX 404, Sarbanes Oxley (SOX) Information for Non-Accelerated Filers,* available at: *www.non-accelerated.com*) setting out the requirements for management and audit reports for organisations with a worldwide market value of under $75 million.

The provisions of the Act are extremely complex and the consequences of non-compliance are equally serious. Any organisation concerned to establish whether it is caught by a requirement to comply with the Act, and then subsequently to meet compliance requirements, should seek professional advice in every case.

18: Risk Management Strategies

The key provisions which apply to listed companies, and to which subsidiary UK companies should have regard, are broadly summarised below.

- Section 302 prescribes the content of periodic statutory financial reports and requires certification of full and truthful disclosure, including deficiencies in internal controls and issues that may have an adverse impact.
- Section 401 requires financial statements to be accurate and include material off-balance sheet liabilities, obligations or transactions.
- Section 404 requires publication in annual reports of the scope and adequacy of the internal control and financial reporting and their effectiveness.
- Section 409 requires disclosure to the public of material changes in financial condition or operations.
- Section 802 imposes penalties of imprisonment for acts committed in respect of financial records with intent to obstruct a legal investigation.

Basel Committee

In February 2003, the Basel Committee of the Bank for International Settlements published *Sound Practices for the Management and Supervision of Operational Risk* to address risk issues in the banking sector. This provides guidelines for good practice in the areas of:

- development of an appropriate risk management environment;
- risk management procedures;
- the roles and responsibilities of supervisors;
- risk disclosure requirements;

18: Risk Management Strategies

- operational risk (which would include risks associated with outsourcing).

Further details are available at *www.bis.org*

Financial Services Authority

The FSA periodically publishes guidance and white papers, on outsourcing issues, in its publications relating to systems and controls, suggesting good practice, including that organisations should not undertake the outsourcing of important operational functions in such a way as to impair the quality of its internal control. Further details are available at *www.fsa.gov.uk*.

These three sources introduce compliance provisions which relate to the financial services sector. The importance of the provisions lies both in their regulatory enforceability, and also in their alignment with principles of good governance and risk management. The compliance provisions set out principles of risk management that might usefully be applied to all financial considerations in an outsourcing project.

Contract finance

Sound financial decisions must also be made in respect of the contractual responsibilities of the organisation. Financial obligations under the contract should be accepted on the basis that an outsourcing project will continue for several years and that they, therefore, might remain unchanged for a lengthy period. Below are key contractual considerations for an organisation in terms of finance.

18: Risk Management Strategies

- **Cost:** the formula to be calculated regarding payment for the services provided, for example, whether per unit, or by total cost of provision, with account taken and allowances made for potential changes in trends.
- **Pricing:** the formula to be adopted for pricing the provision of the services, for example, whether by fixed price or variable rate-based pricing, or a combination, the time and materials involved and the necessary expenses incurred.
- **Payment:** necessary allowances for changes in end-user requirements during the project; facilities for negotiating price reductions; allowances for increased supplier fees for improvements in the services provided; realistic comparisons with similar services.

Other considerations include:

- payment of taxes;
- payment of insurance premiums;
- fluctuating exchange rates;
- the timing of payments;
- delays in payment;
- reservation of the organisation's right to audit;
- payment for implementation of an exit strategy.

Over a period of years, the costs to which these considerations give rise will involve significant amounts. If overlooked, misunderstood or underestimated, the cost to the organisation might bring into question the whole viability of the project leaving the organisation contemplating a costly exit strategy.

18: Risk Management Strategies

Auditing procedures

Another tool in the organisation's financial risk management strategy is the audit. The organisation needs to satisfy itself that the supplier's claims of financial security are supported by audit procedures that conform to recognised standards.

Financial audits

Financial audits check and verify the financial position of a business. They identify financial vulnerabilities and weaknesses and also present opportunities for improving performance.

Audits verify that the processes and procedures for managing the finances of an organisation are sufficient in terms of the effectiveness of their implementation.

A detailed discussion of the financial audit of a supplier in an outsourcing contract is beyond the scope of this book. An organisation should include as a term of the contract that audited accounts are produced by a supplier, to be verified by the organisation's financial advisers as having been audited to acceptable standards.

IT audits

Good governance procedures should include an audit of the supplier's IT services provision under the outsourcing contract.

An IT audit will include IT infrastructure, for instance, hardware and software, systems and networks, data

18: Risk Management Strategies

management (security and confidentiality) and storage, and the performance of automated processes.

Alan Calder[60] suggests auditors should conduct a risk-based audit, usually based on four procedures:

- determining the scope of the analysis of the IT processes by their support of critical business processes and processing of financial information;
- obtaining background information about the supplier's IT environment, its underlying platforms and networks;
- identifying the IT processes which have a direct and important effect on processing financial information; and
- evaluating the effectiveness of each of the major IT processes and related internal controls.

Documented processes, procedures, mechanisms, tools and controls, such as monitoring and reviews, should be available to the auditors. The audit should examine both the infrastructure as a whole and specific applications used by the supplier for provision of the outsourced services.

Specialist IT auditors may be required in order to understand fully the supplier's IT systems and to assess the extent of the audit required. Different types of audit may be needed according to the type of IT in question and to ensure the audit focuses on the audit objectives.

Audit standards

The American Institute of Certified Public Accountants (www.aicpa.org) has developed an internationally

---

[60] *IT Governance: A Practitioner's Guide*, Calder A, IT Governance Ltd, 2005.

18: Risk Management Strategies

recognised standard: *Statement on Auditing Standards* (SAS No. 70) to guide auditors of organisations using suppliers for certain transactions to check the effect on the organisation's financial statements.

Insurance

In view of the wide-ranging and critical nature of the risks arising from IT outsourcing projects, an organisation should investigate the availability of insurance cover.

One underwriter, Pembroke 4000, offers cover of up to £10 million in respect of certain key risks, including loss arising from:

- data loss;
- business interruption;
- the need for data restoration;
- breaches of data privacy;
- damage to reputation and public relations; and
- insecure electronic infrastructure, for example, hacking and extortion, encryption breaches and denial of service attacks.

Chris Newton[61], divisional director of the media technology unit at Pembroke 4000, says that although an SLA may provide warranties and indemnities, in practical terms, the sums recoverable under service credits are often inadequate. He advises that any organisation undertaking an IT outsourcing project should take some basic steps to reduce risk.

---

[61] Interview: 18 June 2009.

18: Risk Management Strategies

First, the organisation must make sure that any steps it has taken to protect its data are mirrored by the supplier.

Second, the organisation should perform regular, physical, professional audits of the security of the supplier's data systems. Many organisations mistakenly assume that the supplier will perform this automatically.

Third, if the supplier's personnel are being employed to provide the service, the organisation should ensure they have the right skills, qualities, ability and competence and that an employer's fidelity bond operates.

Fourth, the organisation should ensure that any due diligence exercise addresses such issues as:

- the adequacy of the supplier's data recovery procedures;
- the supplier's HR policies;
- the involvement of any subcontractors; and
- the use of the organisation's data by any other party and any measures taken in respect of data security.

The organisation should always bear in mind that in outsourcing its IT facilities, it is placing a vital business asset in the hands of a third party and so it is essential that it knows as much as possible about the supplier and that a spirit of mutual trust is developed.

One other area that is considered of importance is the retained IT department. Chris Newton adds:

The organisation must ensure that it retains or recruits adequate and competent personnel to manage the project. These skills will not necessarily be IT skills. They will be managerial and administrative. I would suggest there must be personnel with expertise in finance, risk, contract and SLA management, at least, as well as some knowledge of data security.

So far, Newton says that he is not aware of any claims having arisen from Cloud computing projects. He recognises that the informality of Cloud computing raises additional risks. 'Organisations should make sure that any

18: Risk Management Strategies

security measures employed are as robust as possible and ensure adequate business continuity and disaster recovery procedures are in place', he says.

CHAPTER 19: CONCLUSION: THE GOVERNANCE IMPERATIVE

The adoption and deployment of efficient, cost-effective and modern IT systems is critical to the effective performance of every organisation. As global markets have emerged and developed, competition has become fierce.

The pressure on boards of directors to satisfy the interests of stakeholders by delivering strategies that provide first-rate business performance and adequate profits is continually increasing.

IT is one of the most important tools in the armoury of the board. Adopted, deployed and managed efficiently, IT can revolutionise the performance of an organisation almost overnight. IT introduces new ways of working by automating costly and labour-intensive processes enabling organisations to turn unprofitable activities into highly successful and profitable volume production.

This is occurring in trades, industries and professional service organisations of all descriptions. Lawyers are beginning to face competition from volume providers of conveyancing services which, for so long, have been the preserve of lawyers who claim that this is a highly personal service. Yet, case management systems now automate a wide range of the component parts of the service, making the provision of conveyancing services – and other areas of legal practice – an attractive proposition for service providers interested in the commoditisation of legal services. When these services are more widely available, the whole model of the provision of legal services is likely to change fundamentally.

19: Conclusion: The Governance Imperative

This is just one example of the dramatic effect that IT can bring to bear on the way commerce, industry and the professions provide goods and services.

Many organisations have been content to establish an in-house IT department to manage the needs of the organisation. The IT department has never been a popular resource within organisations, many of the directors and personnel of which do not fully embrace IT and see it as a necessary evil.

Others regard the IT department as an expensive overhead, importing expensive hardware and software, the operation of which they do not understand; employing personnel to rectify faults; and repeatedly exerting pressure to increase the IT budget with upgrades and exorbitant licence fees.

Against this backdrop, the unloved IT department has been expected to react with agility to rapid changes and developments in a global marketplace, facing competition for market share from multi-national enterprises; while, at the same time, striving to meet the needs of increasingly demanding and sophisticated stakeholders who seek profit; and of end-users who demand ever-improving goods and services at reduced cost.

Faced with this proposition, it is small wonder that boards of organisations are urgently seeking alternative business models for the use of IT that will produce maximum opportunity for the achievement of business objectives at minimum cost. Boards require an IT function to enable their organisations to: respond to market needs; compete in the marketplace; provide better goods and services; reduce costs; serve volume markets; serve specialist markets; introduce efficiencies; and, most importantly, enable the organisation to execute its business strategy effectively.

19: Conclusion: The Governance Imperative

Many boards of directors are concluding that compliance with these requirements is becoming an increasingly difficult, if not impossible, proposition for in-house IT departments. Inadequate resources, inability to engage personnel with sufficient skills, global competition and the cost of operating the department have persuaded many organisations to give up the struggle.

The model to which organisations are turning increasingly is the outsourcing of part or whole of an IT function to a specialist supplier of IT services. Specialist suppliers who can host a wide range of IT functions and supply IT services 'on tap' for a fixed subscription are seen as a solution to the shortcomings and inadequacies of the in-house IT department.

Boards view suppliers as specialists in the IT market who are well placed to address all the problems that an in-house IT function presents. Specialists in the market: have access to the latest IT; can access resources at lower cost; can cater for niche markets; can address the needs of volume markets; can master the operation of IT functions effectively and efficiently; and can enable the organisation to achieve profit margins without the problems presented by an in-house IT function.

However, probably most attractive to the board is the fact that outsourcing the IT function divests, or so it seems, the entire management and organisation of the IT function to another party. A key management function for which the board may have little time or enthusiasm can, at last, be delegated to a supplier who can be held to account. In short, outsourcing is seen by many as a panacea for all ills.

Just a brief overview of the features of the model of outsourcing an IT function will demonstrate that the

19: Conclusion: The Governance Imperative

adoption of such a superficial approach is unwise, if not dangerous. The IT function is a business-critical operation for almost every organisation. As it becomes ever more sophisticated, IT will become far more than simply a tool for more effective business performance; it will be fundamental to organisations' very existence.

The operation of outsourcing involves entrusting this function to an independent supplier, probably unknown to the organisation, in the hope and expectation that the supplier will provide a service that will increase the organisation's competitive performance and address stakeholder and end-user interests. This act of faith in the supplier effectively hands over control of a function that is likely to be vital to the organisation's survival.

In doing so, the board exposes the organisation to a host of risks to which it might never have been exposed with an in-house IT function. Just a few examples include:

- business performance risks arising from periods of service downtime, excessive charges, and the employment of unskilled personnel;
- legal and compliance risks arising from the mishandling of the organisation's data, resulting in criminal and civil proceedings and damage to reputation; and
- financial risks arising, most notably, from the insolvency of the supplier.

These examples alone are surely significant enough to cause any board of directors to pause for thought.

If undeterred by the possibility of such exposure, the board should consider what the process of outsourcing actually involves. It is a process that has the potential to expose the

19: Conclusion: The Governance Imperative

organisation to considerable vulnerability across a range of activities.

The board must ensure that its strategy and its supporting business case are feasible and that outsourcing the IT function is a project that supports its business objectives. If the project is not aligned with business objectives at the outset, or becomes misaligned during the project, the exercise will fail.

Next, the board must consider the implications of the process of outsourcing, in other words, the practical steps in the process, and the cost, time, skills and resources, both in terms of personnel and expertise. Considerable quantities of each are likely to be required for each of the following:

- The tendering process
- Pre-contract negotiations
- Due diligence procedures
- Contract management
- SLA management
- Transition management
- Change management
- Termination.

Add to these the post-operational functions, such as the creation of a retained IT department to supervise supplier performance and management of the relationship with the supplier for the duration of the project. Some of the most common reasons for project failure include: misalignment with business objectives, mismanagement of the supplier relationship and inadequate performance levels. Mismanagement by the board of any one of the stages of the outsourcing process has a high likelihood of resulting in project failure.

19: Conclusion: The Governance Imperative

Nor is the structure for the management of an outsourcing project simple. The project is overseen by the board, supported by senior management teams and a project team. But it may also involve teams for the management of the contract, change, transition, contract termination and, of course, risk. In addition, there will be the composition of a retained IT department suitably resourced and managed by personnel with adequate skills.

It is ironic that, at a time when the management, performance and cost of operating an in-house IT department is proving so problematic for boards of directors, outsourcing is increasingly seen as a solution, regardless of the fact that, arguably, it presents the board with far more, and far more significant, issues to address.

For these reasons, the application of governance principles becomes a vital component of any outsourcing process. Governance is an expression associated with the principles of sound management. It is a set of procedures that become embedded in an organisation's culture – and the culture of every organisation is established and promulgated by the board.

It is the board that:

- sets the strategy to meet business objectives and oversees its implementation;
- establishes lines of responsibility and accountability;
- practises transparency;
- provides value for shareholders;
- addresses stakeholders' interests;
- ensures legal and regulatory compliance; and
- adopts a risk management strategy.

19: Conclusion: The Governance Imperative

It is the board that drives an organisation to embrace governance principles. In an outsourcing project, this entails application of corporate governance, IT governance and project governance principles, and the use of:

- tools, such as British and international standards;
- methodologies, such as PRINCE2®;
- compliance provisions, such as the DPA;
- financial controls;
- dedicated IT solutions for PPM; and
- risk management procedures.

While the project is driven by the board, day-to-day implementation is the concern of those identified in the lines of responsibility and accountability established by the board. These will operate on a top-down, bottom-up basis, so that information and decisions are promulgated at every level throughout the project.

The board's involvement in any outsourcing project is critical to its sound management and, therefore, its ultimate success. Although not concerned with daily operations, the potential risks and vulnerabilities at every stage of the process demand a proactive and 'hands-on' approach that ensures governance principles are applied in key decisions affecting the course of the process.

Governance principles should, therefore, be recognised at all executive levels and the board should introduce a system of training and education to ensure decisions are 'governance-led'.

If the traditional outsourcing model offers a management challenge, the emergence of Cloud computing presents a fresh set of challenges. Cloud computing is relatively embryonic and so the range and scope of the management

19: Conclusion: The Governance Imperative

challenge is yet to emerge. What is clear, however, is that, although based on the same model as outsourcing, the features are radically different.

Cloud computing is anarchic compared with the established processes and procedures of the traditional model. The processes are less structured; there is the potential for numerous multi-tenants to be served by a single supplier; data is stored in vast farms of virtualised servers, from which it may be transferred globally without the knowledge of the organisation.

Formal negotiating processes are minimised as contracts and SLAs are 'issued' to organisations, leaving little room for change. Suppliers of Cloud services sometimes suggest that this model is advantageous in that it speeds up the process and enables the organisation to respond to market pressures more swiftly because of the absence of formality.

In these early days, the board must apply governance principles to any proposal to adopt a Cloud solution. Uppermost in its mind must surely be the risks attached to this comparatively untried model of outsourcing.

Successful management of its relationship with the supplier is a critical factor in the success of any outsourcing project. There are two aspects to this management function: the creation of an ethos of mutual respect, and the more practical consideration of the role of the retained IT department to manage the project from the outset.

In respect of the former, the mutual application of governance principles is surely essential. Governance principles introduce certainty and transparency. Corresponding lines of responsibility and accountability established by both organisation and supplier at the outset

19: Conclusion: The Governance Imperative

ensure good communications, regular dialogue and the early resolution of disputes because of the mutual understanding that arises between the parties. Shared and mutually understood objectives, where both parties recognise each other's responsibilities to shareholders and stakeholders and the importance of risk management, foster good relations.

On a practical level, the retained IT department has a vital and enduring role once the project is underway. The board should not underestimate the importance of the retained IT department. It may be tempted to regard it as a skeleton department concerned only with the minutiae of the project.

The retained IT department needs skills, capabilities and resources for such functions as:

- overseeing the IT services of the supplier;
- serving as an early warning mechanism for emerging risks to the service;
- managing relations with end-users;
- managing innovative IT developments;
- marketing the organisation's needs to the supplier; and
- auditing the supplier's performance.

These various functions require different skills and qualifications – a far more diffuse range of capabilities than will be found in most departments of an organisation. The retained IT department is a vital 'catch-all' or 'long stop' whereby the board is supported in the management of relationships, risk and performance during the project. It is a key area for the application of governance principles.

Gartner's concept of brokerage is also a potential area of responsibility for the retained IT department. The role would be that of a conduit between end-user and brokerage,

19: Conclusion: The Governance Imperative

advising the brokerage of the end-users' current needs and future aspirations and instructing the brokerage to locate the services at the best price possible. Possibly, the organisation would retain the full-time services of a broker for this purpose and it is not difficult to envisage competitive tendering by Cloud suppliers for their services in this context. In that event, the dynamics of the Cloud model are thrown into reverse as the organisation supported by its broker assumes the dominant position in the parties' relationship.

Conclusion

IT develops at a rapid pace. In its stream, it leaves organisations striving not only to master the new technologies but also to integrate them into their business strategy in order to compete in a global market.

The development of IT outsourcing models reflects this. Even though IT outsourcing has been prevalent for many years, organisations are still experiencing a high level of project failure for a variety of reasons, the most significant of which relates to the inadequate application of governance principles.

Yet, as organisations still grapple with the traditional IT outsourcing model, Cloud computing emerges and promises – or threatens – to become a significantly disruptive development in respect of all IT services. This process is a reminder of the anarchic development of the Internet in the early days, when initiatives and novel concepts seemed to emerge daily to add further confusion to an already chaotic and largely misunderstood IT model.

19: Conclusion: The Governance Imperative

For organisations juggling with the need to: satisfy the expectations of end-users, survive, compete in a global market and provide an adequate return for its stakeholders, the prospect of unloading the burden of an expensive, labour-intensive IT function to an expert supplier must seem a magnificent opportunity. However, opportunity comes at a price – the application of sound governance principles.

BIBLIOGRAPHY

Guidelines for Directors, Calder A, IT Governance Publishing, 2005, ISBN 1 905356-07-2.

IT Governance Today: A Practitioner's Handbook, Calder A, IT Governance Publishing, 2005, ISBN 978-1-905356-03-04.

Managing the Risks of Outsourcing, Tho I, Heineman, Butterworths Elsevier, 2005, ISBN 0-7506-6574-2.

Outsourcing IT: the Legal Aspects, Burnett A, Gower Publishing, 1998, ISBN 0-566-07698-5.

Outsourcing - business guide to risk management tools and techniques, Lonsdale C and Cox A, Earlsgate Press, 1998, ISBN 1-873439-61-X.

Successful IT Outsourcing, Sparrow, E, Springer-Verlag London Ltd, 2003, ISBN 1 85233-610-2.

The Truth about Outsourcing, Rothery B and Robertson I, Gower Publishing, 1995, ISBN 0-566-07515-6.

FURTHER RESOURCES

Accredit UK *www.accredituk.com*

American Institute of Certified Public Accountants *www.aicpa.org*

British Standards Institution *www.bsigroup.com*

Cloud Security Alliance *www.cloudsecurityalliance.org*

CobiT *www.isaca.org/cobit*

COSO *www.coso.org*

Financial Services Authority *www.fsa.gov.uk*

Financial Services Reporting Council *www.frc.org.uk*

Gartner *www.gartner.com*

Information Commissioner *www.ico.gov.uk*

International Accreditation Forum *www.iaf.nu*

International Chamber of Commerce *www.iccwbo.org*

IT Governance Institute *www.itgi.org*

ITIL *www.itil-officialsite.com*

Jericho Forum *www.opengroup.org*

National Institute for Standards and Technology *www.nist.gov*

OECD *www.oecd.org*

Outsourcing Institute *www.outsourcing.com*

PRINCE2® *www.prince2.com*

United Kingdom Accreditation Service *www.ukas.com*

ITG RESOURCES

IT Governance Ltd. sources, creates and delivers products and services to meet the real-world, evolving IT governance needs of today's organisations, directors, managers and practitioners. The ITG website (*www.itgovernance.co.uk*) is the international one-stop-shop for corporate and IT governance information, advice, guidance, books, tools, training and consultancy.

Other Websites

Books and tools published by IT Governance Publishing (ITGP) are available from all business booksellers and are also immediately available from the following websites:

www.itgovernance.co.uk/catalog/355 provides information and online purchasing facilities for every currently available book published by ITGP.

www.itgovernanceusa.com is a US$-based website that delivers the full range of IT Governance products to North America, and ships from within the continental US.

www.itgovernanceasia.com provides a selected range of ITGP products specifically for customers in South Asia.

www.27001.com is the IT Governance Ltd. website that deals specifically with information security management, and ships from within the continental US.

Pocket Guides

For full details of the entire range of pocket guides, simply follow the links at *www.itgovernance.co.uk/publishing.aspx*.

Toolkits

ITG's unique range of toolkits includes the IT Governance Framework Toolkit, which contains all the tools and guidance that you will need in order to develop and implement an appropriate IT governance framework for your organisation. Full details can be found at *www.itgovernance.co.uk/ products/519*.

For a free paper on how to use the proprietary CALDER-MOIR IT Governance Framework, and for a free trial version of the toolkit, see *www.itgovernance.co.uk/calder_moir.aspx*.

There is also a wide range of toolkits to simplify implementation of management systems, such as an ISO/IEC 27001 ISMS or a BS25999 BCMS, and these can all be viewed and purchased online at: *http://www.itgovernance.co.uk/catalog/1*

Best Practice Reports

ITG's range of Best Practice Reports is now at *www.itgovernance.co.uk/best-practice-reports.aspx*. These offer you essential, pertinent, expertly researched information on an increasing number of key issues including Web 2.0 and Green IT.

Training and Consultancy

IT Governance also offers training and consultancy services across the entire spectrum of disciplines in the information governance arena. Details of training courses can be accessed at *www.itgovernance.co.uk/training.aspx* and descriptions of our consultancy services can be found at *http://www.itgovernance.co.uk/consulting.aspx*.

Why not contact us to see how we could help you and your organisation?

Newsletter

IT governance is one of the hottest topics in business today, not least because it is also the fastest moving, so what better way to keep up than by subscribing to ITG's free monthly newsletter *Sentinel*? It provides monthly updates and resources across the whole spectrum of IT governance subject matter, including risk management, information security, ITIL and IT service management, project governance, compliance and so much more. Subscribe for your free copy at: *www.itgovernance.co.uk/newsletter.aspx*.

Lightning Source UK Ltd.
Milton Keynes UK
28 May 2010

154867UK00001B/5/P

9 781849 280259